The Heart of Our Music

The Heart of Our Music
Practical Considerations

*Reflections on Music and Liturgy
by Members of the Liturgical Composers Forum*

edited by John Foley

LITURGICAL PRESS
Collegeville, Minnesota

www.litpress.org

Publication of this work was made possible in part by a gift in memory of Kathleen M. O'Brien, a dedicated student of liturgy and an accomplished liturgical musician who practiced her ministry in Washington, DC, and at US Air Force bases throughout the world in partnership with her husband John L. O'Brien.

© 2015 by Order of Saint Benedict, Collegeville, Minnesota. All rights reserved. No part of this book may be reproduced in any form, by print, microfilm, microfiche, mechanical recording, photocopying, translation, or by any other means, known or yet unknown, for any purpose except brief quotations in reviews, without the previous written permission of Liturgical Press, Saint John's Abbey, PO Box 7500, Collegeville, Minnesota 56321-7500. Printed in the United States of America.

Library of Congress Control Number: 2015932167

ISBN 978-0-8146-4852-0   ISBN 978-0-8146-4877-3 (ebook)

Contents

Preface vii
John Foley, SJ

1 With One Voice: The Voice of the Church, the Body of Christ 1
   Columba Kelly, OSB

2 *Vox populi:* Voice of People, Voice of Thunder 14
   Steven C. Warner

3 Essentially Vocal Music for the Liturgy 27
   Cyprian Consiglio, OSB Cam

4 The Spirit Breathes in the Multiplicity of Liturgical Music Styles 38
   Lynn Trapp

5 Reflections on Multicultural Celebrations and the Composition of Their Music 50
   Jaime Cortez

6 Three Judgments, One Evaluation 60
   John Foley, SJ

vi *The Heart of Our Music*

7   Composing for the American Church   75
    Tom Kendzia

    List of Contributors   86

    Credits   88

Preface

This volume of *The Heart of Our Music* contains what we think of as "practical considerations."

Columba Kelly speaks of the voices of the presider, cantor, choir, and assembly as integral parts of a framework that is inclusive of the entire liturgy. Then Steve Warner writes about ritual as the voice of people, the voice of thunder—that is, that our liturgies must fully involve our every human capability, including both the physical and the emotional.

Cyprian Consiglio tells us how liturgical music consists essentially and dramatically of melody—but that it includes also the urgency of rock–and–roll, the soaring crispness of Gregorian chant, the earthy rootedness of African rhythms, and the jubilant freedom of jazz.

Lynn Trapp declares that liturgical music has always been various in its styles, nowhere more so than in our own time. The Spirit must be allowed to breathe through the musicians, the music, the community, and then out to the world. Jaime Cortez reflects on what is needed from ministers in order to put their own individual needs aside and think in terms of the collective needs of the larger church.

In my own contribution, I ask about the required three judgments and the one resulting evaluation that are stipulated by the Bishops' *Sing to the Lord* for music in any mass whatsoever.[1] As a member of the advisory committee that composed that document, I can say that the answer does not come easily. The question I ask is: Who is to make these judgments?

Finally, Tom Kendzia draws lessons from some of the important musicians by whom he has been influenced or with whom he has worked: Fr. Clarence Rivers; Paul Simon; Peter, Paul and Mary; and even the St. Louis Jesuits! From these he has come to understand that music at mass must be powerful yet singable—part of the Mass, yet not something that takes you out of the experience.

Each essay in this volume is thought-provoking and written for everyone interested in liturgy—especially those concerned with pastoral music in the English-speaking world. As I mentioned in the preface to the previous volume, this includes pastors, deacons, liturgists, musicians, ministers of the liturgy, people in the pews, and last, but definitely not least, those interested in the future of Christian worship. The composer-authors in this series have devoted their lives to furthering liturgy, because it is the "fount and apex of the whole Christian life."[2] Everything you will find in this series is a product of discussions and sharings at the yearly meetings of the Liturgical Composers Forum (LCF) in St. Louis. I had the good fortune to establish this forum in 1998, and I was privileged to oversee it until 2011 as part of my work as director of the Center for Liturgy at St. Louis University. Since stepping down from that position I have remained a happy member of the Forum, now incorporated on its own.[3]

—John Foley, SJ

Notes

1. See part 4, "Preparing Music for Catholic Worship," section D, in United States Conference of Catholic Bishops, *Sing to the Lord: Music in Divine Worship* (Washington, DC: USCCB, 2007), 126–36.

2. *Lumen Gentium*, 11; cf. *Catechism of the Catholic Church* 1324.

3. Membership in the Liturgical Composers Forum consists of persons who have composed a representative body of ritual vocal music that is (1) published by a recognized publisher of liturgical music, (2) intended primarily for the Roman Catholic liturgy, and (3) rooted in participation by the assembly.

1

With One Voice
The Voice of the Church, the Body of Christ

Columba Kelly, OSB

The voice of the church is indeed one, for it is the very voice of Christ its head. That voice, however, uses different members of the body of Christ at different times during any given liturgical service. Article 28 of *Sacrosanctum Concilium*, the Constitution on the Sacred Liturgy, states that "In liturgical celebrations each person . . . should carry out all and only those parts which pertain to [his or her] office by the nature of the rite and the norms of the liturgy." During the years since the promulgation of that document, a problem has arisen. In order to attain "full, conscious and active participation," that voice needs to be truly heard! It needs to be heard no matter by whom it is voiced or where in the assembly it is being sounded. Even the voice of an individual, such as that of the priest presider or the cantor, is the voice of the entire body of Christ, head *and* members. On the other hand, the voice of the entire assembly, especially when it responds in speech or

---

* Parts of this essay have been published previously by the author in "Basic Chants for the Assembly," *Custos: Newsletter of the NPM Chant Section* 2 (2009): 11–14; and "Gregorian Chant: The Foundational Sound of Christian Ritual Music," *Sacred Music* 137, no. 4 (Winter 2010): 18–31.

song to the presider or the cantor, has often not been heard as it truly should be heard. The voice of Christ is heard primarily through four organs of his body, the church: the presider, the cantor, the choir, and the entire assembly. Let us look at how that voice is heard in each of these four members of the total body of Christ.

The Presider's Voice

The presider of a liturgical assembly is usually provided with a microphone. The artificially amplified sound allows the presider's voice to be adequately heard throughout the space of the church building. It guarantees that all will hear the gospel, the homily, and the eucharistic prayer. The average church sound system, however, flattens out the overtones and the rich variations in the speaker's voice and reduces the attractiveness of that voice for the listener. More importantly, the communication is in one direction only: from the speaker to the passive audience. In the case of the important dialogues with the assembly, such as the Creed, the preface dialogues, and the Our Father, the response from the assembly is not on an equal footing with that of the presider. A sound system is designed to be a one-way communication that can overpower any other sound source in the room, even that of a crying child!

The Cantor's Voice

In most churches, the cantor is provided with a microphone, whether handheld or from the lectern. I once presided at the Sunday liturgies at a parish in which the entire interior space of the church had been "sound-proofed" like a recording studio. There was acoustical tile on the ceiling, thick carpet on the floor, and thick upholstery on the chairs and kneelers. As a result the voices of the different cantors were reduced to a thin sameness that at times became even harsh and hard to listen to as they strained to put sound into the deadened room. Once again, the communication was one way. The assembly made a valiant effort to sing the response to the responsorial psalm, but from my position at the presider's chair, I could hear only a faint, thin sound coming from the nave of the church.

According to St. Augustine in his homily on Psalm 130, it is important for us that we not listen to the psalmist's voice as though it were that of an individual singer, "but as the prayer of all who are within Christ's body." He goes on to say,

> Being members of his body, they all speak like a single individual; the many are one in him who is one. . . . But this temple of God, this body of Christ, this assembly of the faithful, has but one voice and sings like one individual. . . . If only we want it to be so, it is our own voice.[1]

All this is not foreign to our contemporary culture. We are quite willing to listen to a soloist render our national anthem at a major sporting event while we stand at attention and make it our own.

The Choir's Voice

The choir often has several microphones for different sections of the choir and for the instrumentalists. At another church in which I presided for the Sunday liturgies, a sound engineer was not controlling these microphones. As a result, the microphone for the instrumentalists had been set too loud in relation to that used by the choir, which in turn seemed to be set louder than that of the soloist. The result produced an instrumental solo with the choir and the soloist as background accompaniment! After the Mass I had to ask the singers what the lyrics of the songs were that they had sung. The most serious problem came, however, when they attempted to support the singing of the assembly. The more they tried to help, the less one could hear any sound from the assembly itself. One of the functions of the liturgical choir is to be part of a sound framework that is broad and inclusive of the entire space. It is to be a part of something that is larger than the sound that the choir itself is making. This can happen only in a room that has enough resonance in it to support, at the same time, both the choir and the assembly.

The Assembly's Voice

The best singing of an assembly that I have heard was that made by a crowd at a local basketball game singing out their favorite ritual acclamations. The resonant space of the gym held their voices in the air and blended them into one giant triumphant sound. The cheerleaders did not use microphones to lead the shouts of the assembly. They filled their lungs with plenty of air and launched the sound toward the bleachers. When they supported the crowd's response, their voices did not overpower the crowd's voice but blended into it to create one great voice. The total sound was rich and vibrant. It seemed that it was the building itself that was singing their chants and acclamations!

Unfortunately, not many American Catholic churches have that kind of resonate acoustic. Most of these churches are like the church I served for several months while the pastor was away. On my first Sunday there, I decided to listen carefully to the assembly as it finished singing the entrance hymn. The choir and the instrumentalists could be heard loud and clear, thanks to the sound system and their individual microphones. As I faced the people from the presider's chair, a question ran through my mind: "What's wrong with this sound?" The church was indeed filled with amplified sound from the singers and the instrumentalists, but I couldn't hear anything coming from the assembly itself in front of me. In fact, I noticed that most of the people were simply watching the musicians as they sang and played the entrance hymn; they hadn't even opened the hymnal that was in their pew rack!

It was then that I decided to sing the opening dialogue, "The Lord be with you," on a straight tone without accompaniment. There was an awkward pause, and then a few brave souls sent back a timid, "And with your spirit!" The look on the faces of many in the assembly seemed to say, "Are we supposed to sing that all by ourselves?" It was only then that I realized that they had never heard their own voice as an assembly in this church space! Yet I knew that these were among the same people who the previous weekend had sung their hearts out at the basketball game. In the resonant gym space, they produced a unified sound that filled the space as if it were the voice of a single person. Now, in the dry, dead acoustic of this church space, their voices did not combine to form a single voice, but each voice remained weak and isolated in its own separate space in the church.

Usually, the presider, the cantor, and the choir have been provided with a sound system to overcome the dry acoustic that is to be found in most of our churches. Only the assembly is left without any aid to support its voice. Even these sound systems, however, do not provide what a good recording studio has available. In another church where I presided at the weekend Masses, the people complained to me that they had spent a lot of money on the purchase of a good pipe organ for their new church, but after it was installed they thought that it sounded like a bunch of cheap tin whistles! They also complained that the assembly refused to join the choir in singing the hymns at Mass. I suggested that they remove the sound absorbent material from the ceiling and the thick carpet that covered the entire floor of the church. A year later, I found out that they had done just what I had suggested. As a result, they discovered that they really had a great sounding pipe organ. The assembly also began to enjoy singing and hearing its own voice in the building.

What kind of voices are these?

The voice of the church can be that of an individual voice singing to us the very words of God in a sung scripture reading, or the verses of the responsorial psalm. That voice may be very sweet and polished, as in the case of a trained soloist who brings to life some of the deeper meanings of the words she or he sings. That is something that the mere spoken word cannot do. At other times, it is a dialogue between the voice of the presider and that of the entire assembly, especially in the case of the preface dialogue and the Sanctus as the response to the preface itself. In fact, the celebrant alludes to that last part of the dialogue when the eucharistic prayer continues with the words: "Father, you are holy indeed." At times, that voice of the assembly in its responses may be the rather rough-cut voice of a small parish responding to the presider's opening prayer or the preface dialogue. At other times, the voice of the church is that of a skilled choir of singers who lift up our minds and hearts in a beautiful choral setting of praise to God. That voice is the result of combining some individual voices from the assembly who have developed their gifts of music and blended them under the leadership of a musical director. The choral voice they produce is greater than the sum of their individual voices, no matter how good each one individually may be. It becomes a symbol in sound of the mystery of the church.

What makes for "voice-friendly" music?"

Chant was the Roman liturgy's first truly "user-friendly" music for the human voice. It has its roots in the use of heightened speech inflections by someone who wants to communicate firm convictions about something. For Christians, it was speaking boldly about their belief in the risen Lord Jesus. The musical rhythm of chant is inspired and shaped by the sounded words of a good speaker in a large assembly. If you can speak the text with good projection of the voice, clear pronunciation, and intelligent phrasing, then you have most of what you need to sing a piece of chant, whether it be in Latin or in English. As in good speech, each word accent is given its due intensity, while all the other syllables flow rapidly and lightly either to or from that accent. The singer will have the feeling of a pendulum swinging from one accent to the next until it comes to a stop at the end of a phrase. Before the Second Vatican Council, such techniques for speaking in public were to be found only in college courses on public speaking and in monasteries and convents of religious where prayer in common was a daily event. Now every parish is encouraged to train its lectors and singers in the art and techniques of good public speaking. In *The Ministry of Lectors* James A. Wallace remarks: "Rushing through a reading is a very frustrating experience for a listener. And if the pace is at a breakneck speed, people will turn off." He goes on to say: "Put the words together that need to be linked in a 'thought phrase,'" which holds the words together that need to be grouped according to the sense of what is being said."[2] For presiders, lectors, and cantors who would like a more thorough presentation of how to speak together in public, I recommend *Getting the Word Across: Speech Communication for Pastors and Lay Leaders* by G. Robert Jacks.[3] When our presiders, lectors, and cantors present a good model of speaking and singing in public, then their parish assemblies will be able to learn that same art of good speaking. This came home to me after I had experienced the contrast between a parish that had learned to speak as an ensemble and one that had not learned to do so. In the latter parish, I heard the entire Creed recited in one breath! I found myself dropping in and out of the recitation to catch a breath as I struggled to keep up with the assembly. Needless to say, the text was almost totally unintelligible. The first parish had learned to recite a text together, thanks to the good modeling of the presider, the cantor, and the choir members who had been trained in the art of public speaking.

In their instructions for singing chant, the monks of Solesmes now state that "the [performance instructions] given here flow from the perfect correspondence of a sacred text to a Gregorian melody. It is for this reason that singers who show respect for the Latin diction, by that very fact already possess the greater part of what is required to execute well a Gregorian piece."[4] Dom Daniel Saulnier gives the following chant as an example of this. Although each syllable of the word *benesonantibus* has only a single square note, each syllable has a different value and function in the word:

8 *The Heart of Our Music*

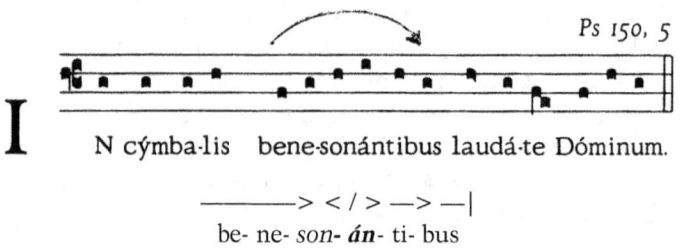

————> < / > —> —|
be- ne- *son- **án**-* ti- bus

The first three syllables are pre-tonic syllables that pick up speed and volume as they accelerate toward the accented syllable. After this buildup, the accented syllable now contains a great deal of energy and volume/duration. This energy and momentum carries through the next syllable, an intermediate post-tonic syllable. The final syllable of the word then absorbs the remaining energy to bring the forward momentum to a closure at the end of the word before moving on again with the following words (*laudáte Dóminum*). The melody forms a Roman arch over the word, a hallmark of the Gregorian chant style of composition. As Dom Daniel Saulnier states:

> The romano-frankish chant shows an entirely new concern for the construction of phrases: the melodic curve in the form of an arch, a . . . concern [that] becomes a canon of composition for the 'gregorian'. The same holds true for the treatment of words. In the case of both the phrase and the word, the Latin accent is handled in the composition by a melodic elevation. Grammar has regained all its prerogatives over the music and finds itself elevated as the *custos recte loquendi* (the guardian of right speech).[5]

The value of each of the square notes in the following example is determined by the value and function of its syllable and the position of that syllable in the structure of the phrase. Once again, note the perfect Roman arch formed by the melody of the phrase:

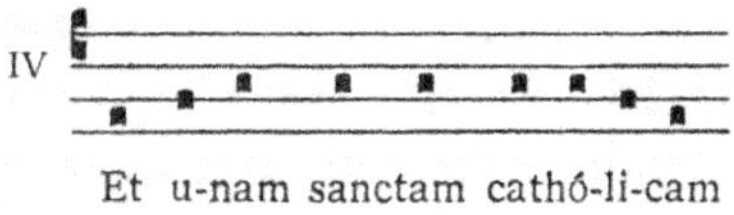

IV
Et u-nam sanctam cathó-li-cam

The earliest chants for the assembly were created with all this in mind. Some of the earliest examples are the Gloria XV and the Sanctus XVIII. The Gloria is nothing but a repetition of a psalm tone formula for each of the phrases:

IV   X. s.

G Ló-ri- a in excélsis De- o. Et in terra pax homí-

ni-bus bonae vo-luntá-tis. Laudámus te. Be-ne-dí-cimus te.

Ado-rámus te. Glo-ri- fi-cámus te. Grá-ti- as á-gimus ti-bi

propter magnam gló-ri- am tu- am. Dómi-ne De- us, Rex cae-lé-

stis, De- us Pa-ter omní-pot- ens. Dómi-ne Fi- li u-ni-gé-

ni-te Ie-su Christe. Dómi-ne De- us, Agnus De- i, Fí-

li- us Patris. Qui tol-lis peccá-ta mundi, mi-se-ré-re no-bis.

The same techniques mentioned above for the lector should be used in singing this English language setting of that same chant. Chants in English should be designed to flow directly from good spoken English. The closer the music is to our native speech, the easier it will be for our assemblies to sing together confidently and prayerfully. If that singing is done in a resonant space, the voices of each individual will tend to blend into one sound. That sound will become the realization of the one voice of the body of Christ, the church.

Text: © 2010, International Commission on Music in the Liturgy Corporation. All rights reserved.
Music: Columba Kelly, © Saint Meinrad Archabbey, 2011. All rights reserved. Used with permission.

The Sanctus XVIII chant is actually an extended acclamation as the assembly's response to the preface that has just been sung by the presider. It flows directly out of the melody used for the ending of the eucharistic preface:

If you know how to speak the language, then you know how to sing these chants! For this reason, the English language setting of the same Sanctus has been given added notes to the first syllable of the first two words in order to allow the proper stress for the accented first syllable and to avoid the danger of letting the accent slide to the last syllable:

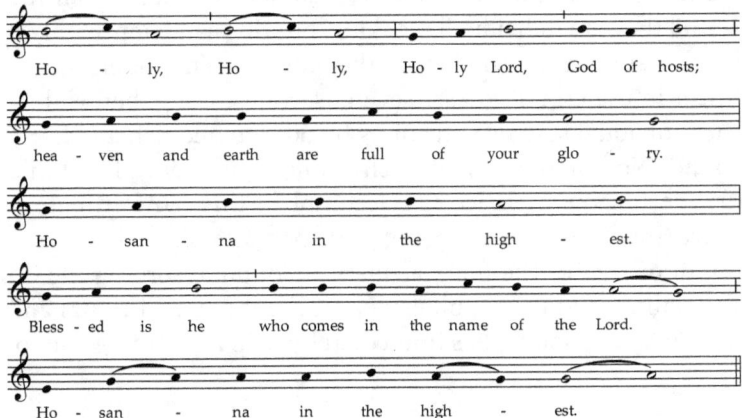

Text: © 2010, International Commission on Music in the Liturgy Corporation. All rights reserved.
Music: Columba Kelly, © Saint Meinrad Archabbey, 2011. All rights reserved. Used with permission.

In the final analysis, the most important element in the production of "voice-friendly" music is the use of a *resonant space*. Organ builders prefer such spaces. The baroque organ builder Arp Schnitger would go into the nave of the church in which he was to build his new organ and clap his hands and sing loudly in order to check the resonance of the space. When asked why he did this, he replied that the sound produced by the building would be the most important stop on his new organ! Choral directors know this very well. They prefer a resonant space for their choir. Many schools have invested in Wenger acoustical shells for use by their choirs when they go on tour. These acoustical shells focus and direct the sound to the listening audience. These modern devices function like the large seashell structures seen behind the pulpits of medieval churches. They produce the focus that the reflector does behind the tiny bulb in your flashlight. Orchestra directors have fought battles with building committees in order to get them to provide enough resonance in a new auditorium for the sake of their orchestra. The sound of a violin string will be only as good as the resonance of the violin casing that acts as its resonating chamber. It is no wonder, then, that a Stradivarius violin is such a valuable instrument!

In summary, the voices of the presider, the cantor, the choir, and the assembly itself have the function of being a part of a sound framework that is broad and inclusive of the entire space. All these voices are to be a part of something larger than the sound they are individually making, but this can happen only if there is sufficient resonance in the building. The sound should linger in the air for at least several seconds. Only then will all the individual sounds and voices blend into one rich and lively sound. No amount of high-tech sound equipment placed in a dry, dead acoustic space can accomplish this. Unfortunately, there are churches still being built or renovated with carpet on all or part of the floor, acoustical sound absorbing tile on the ceiling, and thick upholstery on the individual chairs and kneelers. The sound dies immediately, as in a recording studio.

The lector, the cantor, and the choir struggle to hear themselves, but they cannot. Their voices become harsh and strained. The assembly's voice is thin and weak, for it is not amplified through microphones as are the other singers. Only when the liturgical space has adequate resonance will all the effort at developing good speaking habits and practicing great texts and rehearsing good music be effectively heard. It is just such a resonant sound that is a powerful image of the one voice of the body of Christ singing praise and thanks to our heavenly Father. Then we will indeed be able to hear our true selves—and so will God!

Notes

1. Saint Augustine, "Exposition of Psalm 130," in *Expositions of the Psalms 121–150*, The Works of Saint Augustine: A Translation for the 21st Century III/20 (Hyde Park, NY: New City Press, 2004), 138, 140.

2. James A. Wallace, *The Ministry of Lectors*, second ed., Collegeville Ministry Series (Collegeville, MN: Liturgical Press, 2004), 56.

3. G. Robert Jacks, *Getting the Word Across: Speech Communication for Pastors and Lay Leaders* (Grand Rapids, MI: William B. Eerdmans, 1995).

4. Translated from the Latin of the *Praenotanda* (preface) to the *Liber Hymnarius* (Solesmes: Abbaye Saint-Pierre), 1983), xvi.

5. Daniel Saulnier, review of *Viva voce: Communication écrite et communication orale du IV au IX siècle en Occident latin*, by Michel Banniard, *Études Grégoriennes* 25 (1997): 164.

2

Vox populi
Voice of People, Voice of Thunder

Steven C. Warner

Every January a group of composers from the Western Hemisphere gather to discuss ritual music, theology, and the "state of liturgical art" in the church.

It was at this gathering that I heard a personal credo offered by my colleague David Haas, and it has remained with me since I heard it. "To me," he said while commenting on his role as a writer of song and a musical leader of an assembly, "the most beautiful sound in the world is that of a congregation singing with all their heart, holding nothing back."

"The most beautiful sound in the world." Have you ever contemplated such a superlative? As a church musician, what is the most beautiful sound in the world for you, and how does it fit into your life's work?

In my own work, the above statement about beauty and the congregation's strength of song holds lasting memories in my own heart. There have been moments at Notre Dame—Holy Week, for instance, or the opening hymn for Holy Cross ordinations on Easter Saturday—when the depth of response coming up from the assembly was simply earthshaking. I have witnessed that "most beautiful sound."

An example of this—a memory that might be shared by many church musicians—is what we encountered here on our campus the weekend after September 11, 2001. We chose, at the conclusion of our Sunday liturgy, to sing the noble hymn "O God, Beyond All Praising." After the horror, the blatant evil, and the turmoil of an entire week of despair, we all joined in these words:

> and whether our tomorrows be filled with good or ill,
> We'll triumph through our sorrows and rise to bless
>   you still:
> To marvel at your beauty and glory in your ways,
> And make a joyful duty our sacrifice of praise.[1]

What a radical, prophetic response this was! Battery Park in New York was still in flames, and yet here we were, singing about beauty and glory and triumph. Yet it was exactly what everyone needed to do. And the response was thunderous. It was like an Easter: death would *not* have the last word. Darkness would *not* triumph. The Resurrection—life and hope and love—would win.

What I experienced that day acoustically was not just about mere volume. It was, and is, the kind of singing that embodies breadth and depth and commitment; it conjures forth tears and joys and sacrifice. If you've worked with assemblies long enough, you begin to hear these things in their song.

And when it is unleashed, it is *the sound of the thunder of faith.*

That sound could bring the images of saints, suspended in stained glass, into a tangible dance for joy. The reverberation of that sound might bring the church rafters to tremble for the sonic intensity blasted heavenward. Its strains could catapult the rock of altar and the wood of ambo into something living, for the sheer force of life that is echoing around their corners.

The place of thunder it is.

What does it take to bring an assembly to this place of thunder? What pathways and decisions achieve such a destination? How does one get to this place of response? Does the journey rely entirely on the grace of the Spirit? Surely, all our work is ultimately in the hands of the Holy Spirit—but can our own decisions have a hand in this thunderous creation?

It is critical to examine these participatory moments, stepping back from the vitality and acoustic joy of the assembly. One can move from the ineffable to the effable, putting into words some criteria, a strategy, a plan that might help assure this sacred moment on more than an accidental occasion.

Thunderous response, the full voice of the people, is the result of a fusion of many elements. It is not an accident; it comes with thoughtful planning and a lot of hard work, all of which, when completed, is put confidently into the hands of God. When all these factors come together, when they are not at war with one another but are working together, *then* we have a chance to witness the thunder. It is congregational music making, it is an art, and as my composer friend attests, "it is the most beautiful sound in the world."

What elements affect this music making? They would include (1) the texts, (2) the tunes, (3) the place of worship, and (4) the communal context. Looking at all of these—and extending their considerations to other aspects of the liturgy—might provide a way to get at the mystery and awesome reality of this thunderous response.

Considering these elements, here are a few observations that have surfaced over the past forty years, as we move into our third generation in the vernacular and have now witnessed the new translation of *The Roman Missal*.

Texts

The texts we sing are at the catechetical heart of our spiritual journey. They convey Scriptural truths. They shape our attitudes. They help us glean wisdom from our tradition. Written well, they can succeed in illustrating layer upon layer of our lived faith experience. Once in a hymnal and put out into the mainstream, they gather people together and unite them around a common set of words.

Some texts are shining examples of what our language can accomplish. Others fall short of this mark. Here it is hoped that examples can be provided of both. (It should also be noted that, even when critical of a particular verse or stanza, in no way am I disparaging a lyricist's or poet's entire work.)

When we consider the texts of our sacred songs, is there careful attention given to the accuracy of the theology that we place on the lips and in the hearts of the faithful? If they are doing what they were designed to do, hymns, songs, and inspired songs teach the faith. Is that teaching true? Or do words and phrases occasionally miss the mark? Here is a common refrain of one modern critique: that texts have moved so completely toward celebrating God in one another that they have forgotten that God is eternal. We announce not our own story, but we gather to proclaim *God's* story. It is true that we may see God in one another, but our coming together does not bring God into being. God *is* Being.

Do our texts speak authentically to the ritual action we wish to illustrate? There is a verse I've run across over the years, which states, "Not to preach our creeds and customs, but to build a bridge of care."[2] Is this an accurate expression when placed in the context of Catholic ritual celebration? Part of the identity and mission of the Catholic family is, in fact, to pass along our creed, our prayers, and our ways of doing things. This is the entire reason for the catechumenate. Why, then, does this text state otherwise?

Every word we sing should focus clearly on the ritual action and leave no room for ambiguity. Texts teach. And they teach not only about the tenets of our faith; they help illustrate *why* we do what we do. When, on Easter Sunday, we sing, "You have put on Christ, in him you have been baptized," we are actually teaching ourselves what we are doing ritually. We are being sprinkled with the waters that remind us of our own baptism. We are witnessing the journey of those who stand before us in white garments. We reject sin and its author in this world. The song catechizes, illustrates, what we do in the ritual act.

The fusion between theology and imagery must also be strong and straightforward. Texts convey the truth of our faith, and they must do so with imagery that is neither saccharine nor rooted in the slippery trendiness of pop culture. In many ways, this fusion is the careful responsibility of composers, lyricists, *and* competent editors (who are musicians' greatest friends) carefully looking at every word.

This is not to say that musicians must be straitjacketed by religious tenets, walled up in a one-dimensional and unexpressive world. The best texts are those that open up the religious imagination and are at one with their announcement of the truths of our faith. Here is one such text that shows the wonderful work of imaginative word and theology, fused together in a powerful set of verses:

> From ashes to the living font, your Church must journey, Lord.
> Baptized in grace, in grace renewed, by your most holy word.
> From desert to the mountaintop in Christ, our way we see,
> So, tempted by temptation's might we might transfigured be.[3]

There is so much contained in these two short verses! (The hymn actually has many others as well, with specific verses geared for each Sunday of Lent). The poetic use of "tempting" and "might" are ways in which the lyricist uses the power of word and its creative possibilities to better illustrate the Lenten pilgrimage.

Theological accuracy, ritual focus, poignant religious imagination—all of these contribute to texts that bring us into deeper understandings of our relationship with God. They give us words worth singing, words that will last.

Tunes

It is interesting to watch where our own community at Notre Dame has moved over the past two generations with respect to tunes. Tunes are the canvas upon which our texts are painted; they are vessels that allow us to carry Scripture around, in our hearts and in our minds, day to day and moment to moment. Tunes help us memorize our prayers, our past, our promise.

In the early years of the vernacular, many of our tunes were through-composed—that is, each stanza was set to a different tune. Although they were catchy, there was a difficulty with some of them: Where were the recurring melodic patterns that allowed a person to learn it quickly? What kind of tonal architecture was present? Where was the common formula that made songs easy to own? Even if they were simple, did they hold up to the test of time? And, if the tune was borrowed from another tradition, particularly from another national or folk tradition, was that borrowing appropriate and sensitive to its heritage?

With our own students over the past generation there has been a steady shift toward something old, but something also made new. It is the rediscovery of hymn tunes.

I have watched with great interest as tunes such as *Slane*, *Beach Spring*, *Ellacombe*, and *Bunessan* have made their way back into the mainstream repertoire of both the Catholic parochial and the student liturgical experiences here on campus at Notre Dame. A wealth of folk hymn tunes, many from *Kentucky Harmony* and *Southern Harmony*, have become a steady musical presence within the repertoire of our liturgies, both large and small.

Why is this? Perhaps it is because these tunes have stood the test of time so well. Many are hundreds of years old. Perhaps it is because they are being sought after by poets and lyricists who find in their metrical constructs a worthy canvas for their theological musings. Perhaps it is because, in their utter simplicity, they fit easily into the fabric of liturgy's concise and awesome truths. Perhaps it is because many of them were born out of the tragedy of America's civil war.

And there is one more possibility—perhaps it might be because these tunes are *genre bridges*. They are melodies that can move fluidly between organ, piano, synthesizer, and guitar.

Whatever the reasons, these profoundly simple tunes are reemerging as a canvas upon which to place our theological insights. Here is one contemporary text, wed to the tune *Prospect* from the 1793 collection *Psalms and Hymn Tunes*:

> Now let us from this table rise, renewed in body, mind
>   and soul;
> With Christ we die and live again, his selfless love has
>   made us whole.
>
> With minds alert, upheld by grace, to spread the word
>   in speech and deed,
> We follow in the steps of Christ, at one with all in hope
>   and need.
>
> To fill each human house with love, it is the sacrament
>   of care;
> The work that Christ began to do, we humbly pledge
>   ourselves to share.
>
> Then give us courage, Father God, to choose again the
>   pilgrim way,
> And help us to accept with joy the challenge of
>   tomorrow's day.[4]

If early American tunes seem to be finding a stronger foothold in our liturgy, there are other contemporary elements whose fruit has not been quite so compelling. One such element fit for careful consideration would be "trite syncopation." I use this term advisedly and with sharp focus. By trite syncopation I mean that a piece of music is riddled with the technique. It is, in fact, *overused*, almost unconscious in its appearance in a composition. Syncopation, like any other aspect of putting notes upon the page, is one among many techniques available to the composer. And it can be used effectively, *if done sparingly*. But it is a technique that has a cultural context: it is used pervasively, for instance, in advertisement and pop music. And if this technique is scattered continuously throughout a piece, like any other technique, it wears out in altogether too short a time. It allows the trite into sacred space.

Syncopation is a musical tool associated with songs that are here today and gone tomorrow. Composers would be wise to use this tool with caution, consciously and sparingly. The waters of pop culture are waded when this device is pulled out of the toolbox. How does sacred song, which celebrates God's permanence, benefit from genres that do not stand up to the test of time?

To illustrate this, a consideration of the repertoire of our high school faith music programs might yield some interesting results. Their songs, so far as their own use has shown here on campus, rarely continue for more than a few years, only to be replaced by another set of up-and-coming hits. There is no permanence here—only turnover.

Yet perhaps this is as it should be, for this simple, singable repertoire provides an enthusiasm that will lead the young heart deeper as the journey of faith continues. But therein lies a challenge as well: to coax younger members of the community into an adult faith and an adult faith expression.

At the outset of the liturgical reforms of the Second Vatican Council, the American Catholic Church introduced vernacular songs that, for the most part, have completely been discarded—in some instances only a few years after they were introduced. Yet they set the stage for growth, allowing for another generation of songs that aligned themselves more closely with the richness of Scripture. And with each successive step, decade after decade, the church has actually moved her music toward more eloquent and yet *simpler* forms of expression through litanies, ostinato chorales made accessible by the Taizé community, bar-form hymnody, and now back to chant, both in Latin and in the vernacular. This movement is heartening, for it shows that the noble simplicity of the liturgy has only garnered more integrity with the passing of time.

Here too do our assemblies continue to grow and find their voice; as our texts and tunes mature, our repertoire grows, and the rich diversity of our tradition makes itself more manifest and robust.

Places of Worship

Over the years, as we have moved further and further from the breathtaking days of the Second Vatican Council, some church musicians have bemoaned the reintroduction of chant, both vernacular plainchant and Gregorian, into the liturgy. The source of such whining is not to be explored here, but there is one important question that serves as the background for chant considerations in the Catholic Church, and it is an important one: Can a church dwelling support chant, in the acoustical sense?

For instance, every two years, my ensemble, the Notre Dame Folk Choir, makes a retreat at the Abbey of Gethsemani in Trappist, Kentucky. For any who have visited this wonderful place of prayer, one of the first things of note is the amazing way that music hangs in the air: the reverberation time of this house of prayer is somewhere around five or six seconds. (The joke in our choir is that we can sing a piece and come back the next week to hear it!)

In other words, the church was *designed for chant*. The building supports music that can float, hang, and not be bound by time signature. In fact, metrical settings of sacred song best beware in environments like this. Over the years, I have approached concerts at Gethsemani in a decidedly different way from my first trips to the Abbey. We find ourselves, in our concert repertoire, choosing pieces that have the capacity to "float," rather than ones that move quickly in a strict time signature.

It all comes from respecting the sacred space and knowing what that space demands, musically and acoustically. One of my dear priest colleagues has often said, "Whenever you get into an argument with church space, the church always wins." Wise words are these.

Do our American churches allow for this resonant ambiance? By and large, I think not. And that resonance, that long reverberation, is an intricate part of chant. Our churches, carpeted and muffled, are hardly the places where this delicate repertoire can flourish. Choral directors should proceed carefully when tackling any sort of chant in "dry acoustics," rooms that are compromised with heavy fabrics, cushions, carpets, and the like. It's an integral part of the musical matrix of chant.

And yet, in the absence of a pure acoustical environment, we also have marvelous tools of audio support that may be of enormous assistance to musicians in their labors. This technology too is part of a house of prayer. I've had difficulties, over the years, with musicians who regard supportive, electronic amplification with a puritanical sneer, dismissing the "sheer ugliness of the amplified voice." To those, I would ask: Why then is acoustic amplification used at most major recital halls? Acoustical reinforcement is just that—it is meant to *reinforce*, not overwhelm. Most musicians do not understand that, seeking rather to drown out the voice of the assembly as they assault the assembly with more and more decibels. The result, of course, just like an overpowering organ, is the burying and dismissal of the assembly's voice.

The Community's Context

Every parish has its context: heritage and history, families and failures, personalities and pastoral issues. Every parish also has its *albums:* the faces, the songs, the stories that have shaped its faith journey. All of these, week to week, make their presence known in the way a community celebrates the living presence of God. Mind you, these histories are not the focal point. They are, rather, one of the lenses through which we see God made manifest. It is not our own story that we celebrate. It is the fact that we are part of God's story that brings us life and meaning.

More than one parish musician has made the tragic mistake of moving into a new church and not paying attention to the community—their existing practices, their repertoire, for good or ill—at the outset. They make this mistake at their own peril. A community is on a journey, like the disciples of Emmaus. Jesus knew well to meet them where they were, and not where he insisted they show up. It is a model that all of us should espouse.

This means that even if a bagful of great Easter pieces are at your disposal, it doesn't serve you well to change up a community's repertoire just because you happen to know them, even if they might be better (by your own and others' standards). Know and respect the context of the faithful. This means that rubrics from the past must be respected and revered, at least for the present, even if those rubrics are not as elegant or liturgically poignant as they might be. They can be changed—with time. But first you must meet them where they are.

A church musician's vocation is to enter the parish and learn her or his flock. Our Holy Father, Pope Francis, encourages pastoral workers to "know the smell of their sheep." Jesus did the same, "knowing them as they know me." *Knowing*, in this instance, trumps *doing*. There is plenty of doing to be done, and it will happen, whether we think we're in charge or not (and we're not).

In thirty years of touring with my choral ensemble, we have seen and heard many facets of parish life around the English-speaking world. Some Catholic communities are thriving as never before. Some are in dire straits. Some have priests at the helm who are married (perhaps a sign of things to come), and some are led by truly generous and undaunted lay people, committed to the mission even though they have no ordained leadership on hand. Some have young pastors with many lessons to learn, and some have aged pastors, truly wise and holy men who have been humbled by and cling to the lessons they've learned in life. Our ensemble has moved in and out of these parishes on our yearly pilgrimages, hearing their stories and sharing their joys and their frustrations. We have learned their songs. We have broken bread with them. They've opened their homes to us. We have learned from each other. We have done so *on the road*. This is not just the road of a tour bus—it is the road to Emmaus.

The Thunder

Let us go back to those liturgical celebrations I mentioned at the beginning of this reflection, the liturgies following September 11, 2001. At its heart, this reflection has been about getting to "the thunder," that response from the faithful that brings all things together and makes a community's response something of awe, stirring and powerful.

The theologian and musician Don Saliers once said that people will sing if they have something to sing about. That week in September, when the skies were blue beyond belief and the malice of the world was brought into even sharper focus, all of us sang, maybe better—certainly with more conviction—than we had done in a long, long time. We had something to sing about—of that there is no doubt. We sang to remind ourselves that death would not have the last word.

But, at least in terms of the stance of faith, is there really any difference between that thunder and that of "Jesus Christ Has Ris'n Today," when it is belted out in the dark of the night, having just traversed three days of bread-breaking, tragedy, deception, betrayal, and crucifixion? In both cases, we have something to sing about. In both cases, we remind ourselves—at our Savior's bidding and through his example—that the ways of this world shall not triumph. And our reminders are etched in our hearts with the most significant of tools, that of holy song.

Over the years, there have been musicians—not necessarily church musicians—with whom I have had profound disagreements. The discourse goes something like this: They will say that congregations can enter into full participation while *only* listening. They will say that assemblies need not sing, but just listen. I retort with challenging words, holding out that everything we do in life is relational—even our Godhead is relational—and that as such it must be brought forth in words. It must be celebrated *as Word*. Our God is love, wholly and entirely divine love.

Love has to be expressed. It is not by its nature mute. It cannot remain silent.

Full, conscious, and active: this trinity of qualities, first put forth by the Second Vatican Council, was and still remains the single-most important lens of evaluation for all we do in the liturgical vineyard of the Lord. And besides being excellent parochial compass points, those documents are still the highest liturgical law in today's ecclesial landscape. We would do well to remember this simple fact.

These three attributes—*illam, consciam atque actuosam*—cannot be diminished or misconstrued in their uncompromising vision. Liturgy must fully involve our every human capability—not just the aural sense but the vocal and the visual, the physical and the emotional as well. Liturgy must involve all arenas of our consciousness; it must make deep impressions on heart, psyche, and soul. And liturgy cannot be passive. The documents unyieldingly stress this. Active involvement is the norm.

As a church musician involved in the first two generations of our congregational plunge into the vernacular, every week brings me back to the same questions: "Was it full? Was it conscious? Was it active?"

The thunder happens when we give people something to sing about. We give them texts that are clear, focused, and theologically sound. We provide poetic verse that stirs the heart and captures our imagination and yet is still true to the pillars of our tradition. We paint these precious words with song that has integrity of melody and a noble simplicity that will endure the march of time. We join these words and songs together in a house of faith, using wood and stone and timbrel and reed (and even the carefully adjusted microphone), combining them all together in holy fusion. And we make these sounds in a given place, in a particular family, surrounded by a specific history and a language we know, one that helps us contemplate the mystery.

When all of these elements converge, *thence* comes the sound of the people. And it is the sound of thunder.

Notes

1. Michael Perry, "O God, Beyond All Praising" (Jubilate, 1982).

2. Ruth C. Duck, "As a Fire Is Meant for Burning" (Chicago: GIA, 1992). Note, however, that this verse does not appear in all publications of this hymn.

3. Alan J. Hommerding, "From Ashes to the Living Font" (Franklin Park, IL: WLP, 1994).

4. Fred Kaan, "Now Let Us from This Table Rise" (Carol Stream, IL: Hope, 1968).

3
Essentially Vocal Music for the Liturgy

Cyprian Consiglio, OSB Cam

I want to review briefly the history of Catholic music, and then to suggest that one of the secrets to Gregorian chant's success may be applied successfully to newly written music. That secret is its essentially vocal quality.

The Old Chant

Where did Roman Catholic liturgical music come from before Vatican II? Long ago the official liturgy of the church was mainly set to what today we call Gregorian chant. This chant set the actual words of the liturgy and consisted of a single vocal line without accompaniment from instruments. In Europe, sometime around the tenth century, a new technique called *organum* developed. It was still without accompaniment, despite its name, but another voice was added above or below the original, and the two lines moved parallel to one another. Somewhere around the twelfth century, contrapuntal music (polyphony) began to appear, gradually coming into prominence in the Renaissance era. Added to the chant line were multiple choral voices that moved in harmony but independently of one another. Then instruments began to accompany the voices as well. But the basis of it all was still monophonic chant, the sung text of the rite, though it was often buried under the counterpoint and instrumentation.

Gregorian chant lasted, and indeed continues to live, in various places until modern times. It gave a prayerful experience of the ritual and the official words of the Mass, especially if one understood Latin and could sing the music. Those who did not or could not still enjoyed the beauty of the chant and appreciated its profundity. They usually didn't mind listening to the choir sing more difficult chant pieces and music embellished by polyphony.

In the first half of the nineteenth century, Dom Prosper Guéranger encouraged his Benedictine monks at the famed Solesmes Abbey in France to work on restoring medieval chant. The *Liber Usualis*, containing the complete Latin settings of Gregorian chant for every Mass of the year and many other occasions, was the result of their labors. The monks added markings to the existing chants in order to make it easier for other monasteries (and parishes) to sing.

In my experience, the simple beauty of Gregorian chant is easy to understand if one has experienced it in a "domestic" setting—that is, in certain cultures and communities for whom Gregorian chant is not elite, but rather functional, ritual music. Historically this happened mostly in religious communities, convents, monasteries, and seminaries. The music of the cathedrals was a much different milieu, but one in which chant had its regular place. Chants for both the Divine Office (Liturgy of the Hours) and the eucharistic liturgy are almost exclusively scriptural. Chants for the Office were not difficult except for the antiphons on feast days. Quite often the same settings were used regularly for the Ordinary of the Mass so that they became second nature. Every now and then one hears about a parish that had a tradition of singing Gregorian chant as well, but in spite of the best efforts of Solesmes that seems to have been rare in modern times.

Just prior to the Second Vatican Council many texts and materials were used to teach ordinary people how to sing Gregorian chant. But at the parish level the norm at Mass seems to have been that people sang popular hymns that may not have had anything to do with the liturgical action taking place. The use of hymns in the vernacular had already begun by the early twentieth century, but these hymns were not settings of the actual words of the Mass. They were placed at the four "soft spot" transitions in the Mass: the opening, the Offertory, Communion, and at the end.[1] Only the "Low Mass" could accommodate these hymns, since all of the music for "High Mass" was already prescribed. But the assembly did not sing the ritual itself.

Music at devotions such as the Benediction, Holy Hour, and various Marian devotions became the most popular Catholic music because these devotions allowed for sung participation by the people. Shortly after Vatican II, this hymnic "music of the people" evolved into the folk and popular music that has been so prevalent since then.

If I had been around prior to 1964, I would have been scratching my chin and asking myself, "Is there a way the people could sing the propers and ordinaries of the eucharistic liturgy, and do it with the kind of gusto that they put into 'On This Day, O Beautiful Mother'?"

A famous saying of the Italian liturgist Annibale Bugnini dates from the earliest days of the liturgical reform: "Liturgical song involves not mere melody, but words, text, thought, and the sentiments that the poetry and music contain. Thus sing the Mass, therefore, instead of merely singing during the Mass" (. . . *cantare la Messa, dunque, e non solo cantare durante la Messa*).[2] That's what Gregorian chant did. It sang the Mass, it sang the ritual, it sang the liturgy. So the calls for ritual music that we have rightly heard these past years are hearkening only to our own tradition.

Then came the momentous reformation of the liturgy and its music by Vatican II. It's interesting now to read the following from *Musicam Sacram* (1967) in light of all this: "The following come under the title of sacred music here: Gregorian chant, sacred polyphony in its various forms ancient and modern, sacred music for the organ and other approved instruments, and sacred popular music, be it liturgical or simply religious."[3] I do not think that the council fathers anticipated the kind of musical revolution that was about to take place, at least in the United States. The documents assume that Gregorian chant was going to retain its place alongside other types of music.

What came out of this reformed liturgy?[4] The music of such liturgists as Lucien Deiss and Joseph Gelineau seems to me to have grown out of the old tradition without much interruption. Much of it was inspired by plainsong, based on Scripture, and designed specifically for the voice. Then there were hymns, many of which were borrowed from other faith communities. There was also the folk style, especially in the United States, starting with the era of F. E. L. Publications and artists such as Ray Repp and Joe Wise. There's been some teasing about the "folk scare" of the sixties and seventies, but it is appropriate here to point out the simplicity of this style, its directness, and how essentially *vocal* it was. Many pure melodies and *a capella* music came out of the folk era. Since then we've gone places that no one ever dreamed of—and just about every kind of music that could have been tried has been tried.

The New Chant

Any working liturgical musician knows the mountains of music now available. This is as it should be. We are still in the stage of experimentation. We are still learning how to both sing this reformed rite and sing it in our own language. In addition, we are still learning how to sing it in our own *musical* language, as we are still discovering what that language might be. There is a danger here, however, that we may have already grown comfortable with a mediocre language, a limited palette.

So far this essay has been about chant. With all due respect, and according Gregorian chant its pride of place in our tradition, when I myself speak of "chant," I do not think only, or even mostly, of Gregorian chant; I think of the newly developed chant that has sprung up since the council and chant traditions and styles from parts of the world other than western Europe. I want to state very clearly, so there is no doubt, that I do support knowledge of a minimum repertoire of Gregorian chant, and I love and respect the tradition. But Vatican II called us to go beyond that. A return to Gregorian chant is not the solution to the liturgical-musical challenges of our day and age.

Rightly or wrongly, I have based my thinking about this topic on a rarely quoted text from the 1974 "Letter to Bishops on the Minimum Repertoire of Plain Chant" by the Sacred Congregation of Divine Worship.

> Where vernacular singing is concerned, the liturgical reform offers a "challenge to the creativity and the pastoral zeal of every local church." Poets and musicians are therefore encouraged to put their talents at the service of such a cause, so that a popular chant *may emerge* [emphasis mine] which is truly artistic, is worthy of the praise of God, of the liturgical action of which it forms part and of the faith which it expresses.[5]

First, this paragraph is about the voice—vernacular singing, in particular. Everything else that is musical is at the service of the singing, such that a "popular chant" may emerge. Twice during the 1990s, some friends and I convened a "Symposium on Popular Chant" at our monastery in Big Sur, California. We came up with this working definition of chant: "essentially vocal music"—that is, music that is not dependent on harmony, rhythm, or accompaniment. It could be harmonized and have rhythm and/or accompaniment, but is not dependent upon any of those. We added that liturgical chant would also need to be participatory and at the service of the Word and ritual.

Perhaps this is how people themselves can sing the ritual, as Annibale Bugnini said in 1964. We may get distracted by all the talk about styles of music, the nine paradigms, folk versus classical versus Gregorian chant versus ethnic, even guitar and piano versus organ. But the primary questions are really: What music will support people singing the Mass? What will put the voice out front? What music will sing the ritual and sing the Word?

This is one reason why studying other sacred religious traditions can be so fascinating, especially any tradition in which the music is essentially vocal. The more one studies other traditions, especially those outside of Christianity, the more one finds essentially vocal music at the heart of ritual. I have visited various ashrams and temples in India, and I have stayed with Christian monks there. What I envied was that they have music independent of instrumentation. How the text shines! And we are a text-centered faith, with a Word-centered ritual. (A side note: one danger in focusing too much on "contemporary" worship styles is that the more we rely on sound systems and electric instruments, the further the voice can recede into the background, and with it, the Word, reduced to a mere adjunct to the accompaniment.)

A second thing to draw from that one simple paragraph: "so that a chant may emerge." What a beautiful word, "emerge," which means to me that it is intended to come forth organically, as if it is born. That's a beautiful pastoral image—not that a new chant may be imposed, but that a new chant may emerge. *Sacrosanctum Concilium* makes the same point in another way:

> In certain countries, especially in mission lands, there are people who have their own musical tradition, and this plays a great part in their religious and social life. For this reason, their music should be held in proper esteem and a suitable place is to be given to it, not only in forming their religious sense but also in adapting worship to their native genius.[6]

What does "native genius" mean? Perhaps we may think here of the music of the First Nations. And of course how many Irish people passed through Ellis Island with the tunes of the Celtic tradition still fresh on their lips? Appalachian *a cappella* melodies with their haunting simplicity can be thoroughly captivating. And are not the spirituals that grew out of the marriage of the peoples of Africa with Christianity the root of all our popular music? What about the American Shaker tradition? And in Alaska, what about the Alaskan Yup'ic tradition of chants with drums surrounding the potlatch?

So while I do think an essentially vocal music best serves the ritual, I don't believe that Gregorian chant is the only or best solution for those who want to "reform the reform." It is one solution, and a valid one at that. But we must discover some alternatives and show that other chant forms have evolved and are evolving that carry the weight and fulfill the *munus ministeriale*—a term favored by Fr. Deiss to refer to the ministerial function of liturgical music. Otherwise we will be left with a very uncreative response to the challenge of Vatican II: "Let [composers] produce compositions which have the qualities proper to genuine sacred music . . . which make possible the active participation of the whole congregation."

Could we let the Gregorian tradition serve as a signpost for us in its preference for and cultivation of an essentially vocal music for the liturgy? Gregorian chant *is* an essentially vocal music that appreciates the voice as the main instrument of liturgical music. It *is* an essentially vocal music that serves the text well, with the least amount of interpretive supplementation. And it *is* an essentially vocal music that also fits smoothly with the rite as it gently flows in and out of the spoken word.

Sources for a New Chant

In the antechambers of the liturgy, outside the church, something fascinating is going on. People are finding spirituality, spiritual practices, and ways of living that would put us to shame in terms of its integrity, dedication, and transformation, and they are doing it without the church—and sometimes in spite of the church. At times they may be misdirected, solipsistic, and looking for easy answers and a certain permissiveness in their own way, but they are not afraid of the sacred. They are not afraid of asceticism, of sweat lodges, or of sitting hours in meditation, fasting, reading sacred scriptures, and building a way of life that reflects their spiritual values based on peacemaking, love for the earth, mental health, and care for the body.

I'm fascinated by the sacred music from around the world that they are listening to: music of the Native American tradition, music from Africa, Tibetan chanting, Sufi *qwali* singing, and Indian *bhajan* singing. As a matter of fact it's mostly what we would describe as chant (or at least as what I would describe as chant): essentially vocal music that may be rhythmic or harmonized, but is not dependent on either. It's essentially vocal.

This is an audience that will not be satisfied with a music that is not technically, aesthetically, or expressively *good*, or that is cheap, trite, or a musical cliché as often found in popular styles. This is the audience that helped make such a huge success of recent albums of Gregorian chant and the music of Hildegard of Bingen.

Robert Gass has put together a great CD collection and book on chant, in which he describes and presents chants from traditions all around the world.[7] I assumed that if he included Christian chant, it would be something Gregorian, but no: he picked the music of Taizé as the type of chant that fits in best with the other chants he describes.

Composers have drawn from pop music, folk music, classical music, and Broadway shows, but there are other places that we are not completely exploring in our search for our own voice in liturgical music. Perhaps in this era liturgical composers and musicians should also be studying with Hindu *bhajan* singers and the Brahman priests who sing the ritual and have committed the Vedas (the Hindu sacred scriptures) to memory; the Jewish *hazzan*, who is not only the cantor but the guide of the synagogue celebration; the Muslim *hafiz*, who commits the entire Koran to memory; perhaps listening to Buddhists chant a sutra or their dharma lineage together at the end of a period of meditation.[8] Why? From a practical standpoint these are types of music that sit gently on a rite and give pride of place to the word (if not "the Word"). From a theoretical standpoint, somehow I get the feeling that these musicians are doing the same thing that we are trying to do, and that our music comes from the same root: this challenge of daring to give voice to the sacred.

I am not suggesting that we should be singing Indian *bhajans* or *qwali* music in Western liturgies but rather that these may help us find our own voice. I don't sing Hindu *bhajans* so that I can be a Hindu, be an Indian, or sing like an Indian; but somehow Indian music helps me find my *own* voice in proclaiming a sacred text in song. Most European Americans, for example, are never going to be able to sing gospel music or spirituals as naturally as African Americans. But I'm not trying to sing like an African American; what my week with Clarence Rivers and Grayson Brown in 1977 did was to help me find my voice through that music. Taizé music sometimes comes under criticism; one composer loves to tell me he thinks it's not good music, and another liturgist wrote that we should not be imitating French monastic music. But again, the point is that Taizé helped us find our voice. It helped us discover a simple thing like the use of the ostinato in worship to sing Scripture in praise, and it aided our rediscovery of the litanic form in a fresh new way. And it is a music that emerged. It worked! People love singing it, and that alone yields its own lesson. If we were to combine the soulfulness of gospel music and spirituals with the devotion of Hindu *bhajans*, the contemplative presence of the music of Taizé with the sturdiness of the Gregorian liturgical sensibility, we would be worshipping God as thoroughly human beings.

I think the music of John Bell and the Iona Community provides another example. Their music, even their experiments with music from around the world, is not stealing, and I don't think the word "hybrid" works either. It is music that has emerged out of a living and breathing worshipping community that is committed to the Word, to sound liturgical principles, and to stepping unashamedly into new musical territory.

One last example that interests me as a liturgical musician is the ECM recording label founded by Meinfred Eicher out of Munich in 1969.[9] In my words, what they are doing is combining classical, jazz, and world music; perhaps better put, they are not discriminating between these genres, but rather producing a marvelous new synthesis. One example is the great jazz pianist Keith Jarrett playing the Shostakovich preludes. An even better example is *Officium*, the beautiful and popular recording by the jazz saxophonist Jan Garbarek, who improvises while the Hilliard Ensemble sings sumptuous Renaissance polyphony. Here are some of the liner notes from that recording:

> When jazz began, at the beginning of this century, it had no name; nor did polyphony when it began a thousand years earlier. These two nameless historical moments were points of departure for two of the most fundamental ideas in Western music: improvisation and composition. . . . What is this music? We don't have a name for it: it is simply what happened when a saxophonist, a vocal quartet and a record producer met to make music together.[10]

I have for some years been interested in the common ground that may be found between jazz and chant—not in the interest of having a jazz Mass, but in the interest of our voice emerging out of our native genius. Along with all the other resources available to the aspiring liturgical musician today, I recommend the first episode of the Ken Burns *Jazz* documentary series, "Gumbo," which explores the combination of elements that went into the birth of that new art form. Classical music, band music, African dances, and spirituals all combined in the New Orleans of the late nineteenth and early twentieth centuries. This is part of our native genius—the roots of our pop music, gospel, blues, and rock. The point is not to have a rock Mass, or a blues Mass, but rather that *from our native genius*, out of our "gumbo," a popular chant may emerge.

Where would we be if our music and our church really reflected the native dispositions of the human voice and its rhythms? The result might not be neat and clean, but it might have the urgency of rock and roll, the soaring crispness of Gregorian chant, the earthy rootedness of African rhythms, and the jubilant freedom of jazz.

What would we call this music? We don't have a name for it
. . . but I believe it is emerging.

Notes

1. The terminology of "soft spots" was developed by Robert Taft, SJ, to refer to those places within a ritual that were not yet canonically "hardened" and that were therefore open to insertions or increments. See Taft, *Beyond East and West: Problems in Liturgical Understanding* (Washington, DC: Pastoral Press, 1984), 161, 168.

2. Notitiae 5 (1969), *Documents on the Liturgy 1963–1975: Conciliar, Papal, and Curial Texts*, ed. Thomas C. O'Brien (Collegeville, MN: Liturgical Press, 1982), 406.

3. *Musicam Sacram*, 4b.

4. John Foley, SJ, *Toward Ritual Transformation* (Collegeville, MN: Liturgical Press, 2003), 109–28.

5. Sacred Congregation of Divine Worship, *Voluntati Obsequens* (A Minimum Repertoire of Plain Chant), April 14, 1974. Online at http://www.ewtn.com/library/curia/cdwplain.htm.

6. *Sacrosanctum Concilium* 119 [emphases mine].

7. The book is *Chanting: Discovering Spirit in Sound* (Boulder, CO: Broadway, 1999); the CD is Robert Gass, *Spirit in Sound: Chant* (Boulder, CO: Spring Hill Music, 1999). The book gives example of what I like to refer to as "popular chant," borrowing the phrase from the above-cited Bishops' letter, whereas the CD contains more solo, virtuosic pieces, including from the Christian traditions various selections of Gregorian and Byzantine chant, and a piece from the delightful music of the Trappists in Keur Moussa, Senegal. As for the latter (and talk about native genius!) there is a beautiful weaving of African Wofol and Mandingo rhythms and instruments with Gregorian chant and scriptural-liturgical texts.

8. The *hazzan* is trained in Hebrew vocal and musical mastery, and is considered to be the custodian of the liturgical tradition. In the orthodox Muslim world religious music is strictly vocal, with no instrumentation, and the *hafiz* learn a highly structured and refined art of chanting, including specified pronunciation, pauses, and phrasing.

9. See http://www.ecmrecords.com/About_ECM/History/index.php for the history of this endeavor.

10. John Potter, liner notes for *Officium*, Jan Garbarek and the Hilliard Ensemble (Munich: ECM Records, 1994).

4

The Spirit Breathes in the Multiplicity of Liturgical Music Styles

Lynn Trapp

It was a Sunday in Ordinary Time, and as I sat in the pew reviewing the printed order of worship before the liturgy, the titles seemed to leap from the page with more interest than usual. There were at least four languages represented by the music titles with translations provided for those. While I was aware that the assembly of this parish was a melting pot, the diversity of the menu drew me closer. As ministers assembled, I noted that the music was under the leadership of a keyboard player and cantor. My interest in the challenge of the liturgical music program for the day heightened my awareness of the great importance of the respect and musical skill required by a music minister to be successful with diverse styles.

The cantor sang an impressive proclamation of the psalm antiphon in both Vietnamese and English, with the verses sung in English. The musician at work had obviously written the syllables of the Vietnamese antiphon to the same melody as the English version, with good success. The song at the preparation of the gifts was from Kenya. The assembly sang the refrain twice each time—first in Swahili, then in English. The verses featured the languages in alternation. Even without percussion the pianist's skill provided a rhythm and style that made each piece successful in its own right, luring the assembly to participate as many tried their best to sing a language unfamiliar to them. The Spirit seemed to breathe through the music and move the assembly to prayer, across any boundaries of language, race, and musical style.

Traveling through the liturgy I continued to be impressed by the skill with which the musicians launched each piece in an engaging style with special attention to articulate language. The organ postlude was a quick-paced allegro by Johann Walther from the Baroque period. It seemed to be just the right cap on a program that was so diverse from the beginning.

I left knowing that my experience was one that had woven prayer and music. The various languages were not an obstruction to prayer, and the multiple styles did not require a different musical ensemble for each in order to be sung successfully. The skill and preparation of both cantor and keyboardist were laudable. I was convinced that the combination of native musical styles in the liturgy can be successful and that it does not have to be Pentecost to have the opportunity to design such a program.

As worship directors, music directors, and composers, do we welcome and support varied styles in the community we serve? Perhaps we have tended to limit the styles of music that are programmed by the agenda, taste, and talent of the one who is in leadership. "Even as the liturgical music of the Western European tradition is to be remembered, cherished, and used, the rich cultural and ethnic heritage of the many peoples of our country must also be recognized, fostered, and celebrated" (*Sing to the Lord* 57).

As we appreciate the diversity in the Body of Christ, those of us in music ministry are called to move beyond ourselves to explore and employ styles that connect to the cultural mix. We keep our fingers on the pulse of the assembly, its participation, and its reaction to style. We make decisions to serve the worshiping community, not to serve ourselves. "Liturgical music must always be chosen and sung 'with due consideration for the culture of the people and abilities of each liturgical assembly'" (GIRM 40). Or, as *Sing to the Lord* puts it: "Liturgical music today must reflect the multicultural diversity and intercultural relationships of the members of the gathered liturgical assembly" (60).

It is our Christian responsibility to foster unity among our diversity in worship. It may be that a particular ethnic group has approached you about incorporating their particular musical style into the worship of the parish. If there are musicians among them, they should be invited to share their musical repertoire in sessions with the parish music director, discussing appropriate liturgical usage and together selecting pieces that can begin to be blended into the parish repertoire. The musicians of the particular ethnic group must be present to launch these pieces with the assembly. This gives justice to the music and provides a point of reference for parishioners as they begin to see the leadership and hear the music of a style borne from fellow parishioners. Perhaps this music will be a first connection for many to an experience of those around them who bring other cultural backgrounds to the parish.

In judging the appropriateness of music for the liturgy, the principles must not be compromised, regardless of ethnic style. Sometimes various ethnic groups will bring an experience from their native land that does not seem to align with the grid on which the liturgy should be planned. With the ultimate importance of texts and their connection to Scripture and season, and with respect to the ritual, the music must always be examined for its liturgical, pastoral, and musical qualities. "All three judgments must be considered together, and no individual judgment can be applied in isolation from the other two. This evaluation requires cooperation, consultation, collaboration, and mutual respect among those who are skilled in any of the three judgments, be they pastors, musicians, liturgists, or planners" (STL 126).

It is important that any new style be articulated with authenticity. A good understanding of the background of the music and how it is rendered in its native country is essential for music ministers in leadership. The delivery must not seem that they are experimenting with the style, but mastering and projecting it for assembly participation. Particular instruments will treat the music with its indigenous flavor. It is best to keep the instrumentation and vocal leadership simple rather than presenting the notion to the assembly that a particular new music can be successful only with a larger specialized ensemble. However, certain elements of the music will have to be maintained in order to remain loyal to its quality. Would the music of Africa be brought to the liturgy without percussion? No. Would the music of Taizé be employed without any interest in layering of voices or instrumental enhancement? No. Should a piece in Tagalog be sung without knowledge of the proper pronunciation of text? No. Musical authenticity requires that certain elements be maintained, and inclusion of music from cultures other than one's own demands that those elements be identified.

As with any liturgical music style, the text must be taught and delivered cleanly, and the rhythm and lyricism of the music must be performed with reverence and respect to both the ritual and the space in which it is being rendered, so that all is engaging to the assembly for participation and prayer.

When parishioners of a particular ethnic music style suggest introduction of the style in worship but there are no musicians among them to offer leadership, it presents a special challenge for the parish music director. The director's awareness of resources within the local community and diocese will be most helpful. An invitation to musicians who can deliver the style well may be invited to share the music with active parish musicians and at worship. However, it may not be possible due to limited resources of budget or other factors to continue their involvement from outside the parish. The director must discern whether or not the parish's music ministers can treat the new style with justice and sustain its value in the worship life of the parish. The ability of the musicians is a factor as well as their willingness to learn and teach a new style, all of which must be encouraged. Under no circumstances would it be appropriate for a recording of music to be played in the liturgy instead of live musicians just to include the style in the parish's worship profile, and to satisfy the suggestion of a particular ethnic group. "Recorded music lacks the authenticity provided by a living liturgical assembly gathered for the Sacred Liturgy. . . . It should not, as a general norm, be used within the Liturgy" (STL 93).

The willingness to be open to experience the Spirit breathing through a multiplicity of liturgical music styles in a parish community may need to be prepared, groomed, and nourished. It may be that a style of music is suggested by a particular ethnic group that represents a very small portion of the parish. When dropped into the liturgy, the new music may seem token, existing in isolation. To shed any misdirected sense of foreign label, it is the responsibility of the music director in both written and verbal forms to communicate with the parish that the music lives within a broader context of parish life. The pastor and other governing bodies of the parish must be supportive as well. Respect for the diversity of the Body of Christ is the responsibility of the entire Christian community.

In order that the parish community may grow to witness the fuller presence of an ethnic group or groups within the parish, a groundwork should be laid within the life of the community for the cultivation and appreciation of diversity among its people. It may be helpful for the entire parish to engage in a task force focused on multiculturalism. This may take the form of a parish retreat, mission, or a series of presentations—whatever plan will inspire the attendance of as many parishioners as possible. To begin, a team of people representing the various cultures of the parish are invited to engage in a program of studying church documents, praying together, and faith sharing. Internally, the members of the group achieve a growing awareness and appreciation of styles of life and devotion among their native countries. They may be invited to bring sacramentals, music, pictures, clothing, or any items that help express their ethnic roots as they share with one another on the team. Choices of assigned reading material assist their education of the church's teaching on diversity. Study questions are provided to cultivate thought and discussion about various aspects of diversity in the Body of Christ. The group collaborates in forming a document with shared points and examples of diversity made manifest in the community. Then the team holds a special time or times of gathering of the parish during which the fruit of the task force is presented by the team. At that time team members present the points verbally with printed copies available for all in attendance. The individual team members' presentation with natural tone and native accent as well as native dress contributes to the aesthetic of the parish gathering. The parish is invited to reflect and comment on the points as they begin to take root within the life and mission of the parish.

A final document with all points of the team and parish gathering is printed and promulgated to the entire parish.

Following are some points that were charted from a task force that I have led.

The universal church has always been multicultural. Through the ages, luminaries in Christian history—popes, bishops, saints, martyrs, great teachers—have come from many corners of the earth, representing many races and cultures.

We must acknowledge that we are a multicultural community. The richness of the community is founded in one faith, one baptism, one creed of the universal church. We must respond to the needs of the community's members and our obligation to the Gospel message to serve one another.

We, the church, need to respect a broader understanding of family. We must embody and live the core values of family. The spirituality of the community is experienced in both large communal gatherings and small groups. All contribute to the life of the larger parish community.

Full expression of a community's varied cultures includes symbol, movement, dress, word, and music. Such varied cultural expressions reflect both the community's strength of identity and its gratitude and thanksgiving for God's many gifts.

The ultimate goal of this type of groundwork is that the parish gains an openness to receive and experience the people and expressions of those in other cultures in the parish community.

The music of the community's celebration will thus have a reference point beyond a token piece in the musical menu of the liturgy. The music will have an integral connection to the spirituality and formation of the community inspired by rather than hindered by race or dialect. Connecting the liturgy and the life of the parish is crucial to the health of the parish, and the education and appropriate implementation of new elements in the musical liturgy are vital to its success.

Once an appreciation of a new style seems to be gaining acceptance and participation within the parish, it will become evident that the experience of growth has provided a new lens from which to view the community and all its liturgical celebration. Too often a parish's music repertoire is comfortable but stagnant. It lies in a rut that may be difficult to reform. The freshness desired may not necessarily be gained from adding new music within the same style of repertoire, but certainly gained from the incorporation and leadership of music borne out of the community's people. It is senseless to introduce a long-term plan for the inclusion of a new ethnic style of music in the liturgy that has no connection to the human makeup of the parish. Sometimes parishes use the liturgy of Pentecost to feature a multicultural menu of music because of the evangelical nature of the solemnity and its theology of "many tongues." Sometimes parishes use the liturgy of the Easter Vigil, the mother of all vigils, due to the many psalms and ritual points that call for music. Both of these great church celebrations may very well be times to employ the musical flavor of various cultures and languages. However, if these exist as the *only* peak times in the parish's liturgical year for this treatment, and if there is neither a further rendering of this music throughout the year nor deeper connection to the cultures of the parishioners, the experience will be merely a token one. It may have been discovered that a house of worship nearby or within the same denomination is trying a type of music and it should be tried in other houses in order to "keep up with the Joneses." The impetus for launching music of various cultures must be borne out of the human fabric of the parish, the people in the pew, the spirituality of parish life. Without this approach, a new cultural music will be experienced as token, a nod to a culture that is not represented by people in the parish, a challenge of song that seems to have no purpose, and will likely bring frustration and even alienation for the worshiper.

There is value in presenting the point that tokenism in music choice for worship today has been diminished due to the development of a broader context of style brought by the combination of cultures. The fact that more music for worship from various cultures continues to be brought to worship expands profile, taste, and acceptance. The very exposure of multicultural music in worship has brought growth to ears that may have once been biased.

In general, houses of worship in the United States are increasingly filled with people of varied race and color. People's expectations of and suggestions for their worship should be cultivated in order that the community may gain an acceptance and appreciation of styles that connect to those around them. Because of the growth of parish populations with varied cultures it is much less startling today to experience music sung in more than one language in a traditionally Caucasian parish than it was before the Second Vatican Council. The council dawned the celebration of the Mass in the vernacular, which brought with it other mulitcultural styles and traditions in worship. Has tokenism in liturgical music disappeared? No, but it has *diminished* because of the broader demographic in which liturgical music currently exists. A movement toward blended worship now exists in parishes in order to attempt to satisfy the need for inclusion and unity in musical worship. There remains, however, an ongoing need for greater understanding and experience on the part of the music director who leads the formation of the program so that no degree of tokenism surfaces.

The notion of blended music in worship, fusing both traditional and contemporary styles into a single service, has reached such successful practice in the church world today that for many communities it has become the norm. Furthermore, blended approaches have affected areas of worship beyond music, such as the leadership style of the minister, prayer texts, scripture choice, liturgical environment, dance, and the decorum of worshipers before, during, and after worship.

Throughout music history the terms "traditional" and "contemporary" have been ambiguous labels. For some, chant is traditional, but because J. S. Bach's harmonic language of the eighteenth century was so progressive, his music may be considered contemporary. For others the symphonies of Johannes Brahms present a classical style that is traditional, and only the music of Leonard Bernstein and beyond is contemporary. For many, contemporary refers to the music of the day written by composers who are living, and traditional refers to music of deceased composers. The range of music that might be associated with these two categories varies a great deal depending on the historical timelines assigned to these categories, musical preference, and one's musical experience as a listener, educator, or performer.

In order to blend styles successfully a worshiping community must work to define what characteristics define the music as traditional or contemporary. It may be instrumentation, text, history, music arrangement, rhythm, volume, as well as many other factors.

People come to worship influenced by a world that boasts both chant and rap music with the expectation that whatever style they like should be represented at worship, regardless of whether the program of music within the liturgy is cohesive. We come to worship from experiences in high school auditoriums and orchestra halls, where musical styles are blended so that the engaging quality of the program keeps people coming back for more. Throughout music history secular and sacred styles have blended. The music of medieval town minstrels creeped into the church transformed with new text for appropriate use. The symphonic music of the classical period was fused with the texts of the Mass, and long movements of Kyrie and Gloria were performed during the ritual of the Roman Catholic Church. Popular love songs with texts about humanity and unity are often suggested for worship regardless of whether or not they mention God or the plan of salvation. Our worship exists in a blended world of culture and taste. Any wall separating world and worship negates the goal of liturgy, which is to connect liturgy and life. It is the job of the ministerial staff to guide the selection of music and the formation of the assembly so that liturgy and life are connected with respect to the principles of the church.

The art of blending styles in worship takes considerable time for study and selection of repertoire that holds quality and theological depth. Each piece of music must be carefully reviewed for its relationship to other pieces within the same liturgy. Elements of rhythm, timbre, key, and tempo must be considered when designing the plan. How do the pieces operate, exist, and communicate alongside one another in the ritual? How do the texts flow from gathering of the assembly through the liturgy of the Word and Eucharist to the mission and service of the church? How does the complexity of musical texture influence the placement of pieces in the ritual? How can the overall balance provide a sense that the musical plan was not strictly and academically situated on a grid, but that the Spirit has given its breath to the structure? Perhaps we try too hard to make all musical choices "match" in a liturgical plan. It may be that the overall experience of a program in which pieces seem matched is not engaging at all and that greater inclusivity and creativity are needed. The Spirit must be allowed to breathe into the hearts of all who sing with their own breath the music and text provided for worship. Then the musical liturgy will connect with life. Then will the flow of the ritual lead one to prayer without hint of race, color, or foreign boundary. Communal prayer ascends. Unity abounds.

Blending styles also includes the technique of articulating a particular genre with instruments that may not usually be associated with that genre. For example, contemporary music ensembles in the parish should be encouraged to include standard hymns in the repertoire. Piano, organ, guitar, drums, percussion, and other instruments can successfully accompany and lead homophonic hymns. The ensemble must be committed to learning how to combine the instruments for the best possible delivery of the music. The hymn must be enhanced with the appropriate rhythm, keyboard accompaniment, and obbligato lines so that the texture does not become too busy and blur the solid leadership required of the hymn. The combination of instruments should certainly vary for the different stanzas of the hymn inspired by the images of the text.

Blending styles can also include the art of placing classical music appropriately in a liturgical music program. At an African Mass celebrated with music sung in more than five native languages, why not close with an organ postlude by a composer from the seventeenth century, such as Dietrich Buxtehude? The idea seems startling, risky even. But there very well may be elements of the organ piece that reflect the *tone* of the overall liturgical experience and provide just the right "sound" for the end of the program.

The organ is too often considered only as an instrument that sustains tone. In addition to playing repertoire, the organ, with its rhythmic capability under accomplished hands and feet, can effectively liven the ensemble alongside a driving percussionist on the trap set. The registration of the organ lends a palate of orchestral sounds from which to choose and contribute to the ensemble sound.

The art and joy of blending styles requires discipline and taste, knowledge of repertoire and ensemble experience, respect for liturgical texts, and respect for all people involved. We must take the opportunity to explore the possibilities before us that bring the music to life so that in combination a musical design of multicultural, multilingual, multistyle can be a successful component of the liturgy.

The principles and examples I have shared here are based on my own experience as concert organist, conductor, composer, and liturgist. As pianist and organist I play all styles from jazz and gospel to Buxtehude. The challenge and joy throughout my career as a parish musician continue to provide the means to bring these styles to worship in a way that is engaging, appropriate, and connected to the community. I present this faithful challenge to you too so that the Spirit is allowed to breathe through the musicians, through the music, and through the community to the world.

5

Reflections on Multicultural Celebrations and the Composition of Their Music

Jaime Cortez

I grew up in El Salvador in Central America. That is where I completed my elementary and high school educations. Due to the painful difficulties of the civil war taking place in El Salvador, however, my family decided it would be best for me to move to the United States to continue my studies. I became an immigrant, and like other immigrants I sometimes felt out of place. Even coming into the US Catholic Church there was an occasional feeling of being *an outsider*.

Then one day I heard this passage from St. Paul's letter to the Ephesians, describing Jesus as "our peace" and the one who "broke down the dividing wall of enmity. . . . He came and preached peace to you who were far off and peace to those who were near" (Eph 2:14, 17). This passage proclaims that we are all one in Christ. From hearing this I understood that no matter where I am I have something to contribute to the church. Whether Chinese or Russian or Salvadoran, we *all* have something to bring and to contribute to the Body of Christ. We have the right to be in church and the right to share our culture with the church. From this pivotal moment on, I knew I had something to contribute to the church from my own culture—even while residing in the midst of a dominant culture.

The implication for liturgical music is obvious. In the church we celebrate all the members and *with* all the members at Mass. This meant to me that when two or more cultures were present at liturgy, it would be ideal to have the tools available to foster everyone's prayer through Word and song. What is commonly referred to as bilingual or multicultural music has emerged in order to help us do just that. On this basis I suggest that the church today must be open to two dynamic truths: first, that the entire worshiping community is *enriched* by the presence of multiple cultures and that, second, we enrich *other* cultures by sharing our own.

The First Steps

> For he is our peace, he who made both one and broke down the dividing wall of enmity, through his flesh, abolishing the law with its commandments and legal claims, that he might create in himself one new person in place of the two, thus establishing peace, and might reconcile both with God, in one body, through the cross, putting that enmity to death by it. He came and preached peace to you who were far off and peace to those who were near, for through him we both have access in one Spirit to the Father. (Eph 2:14-18)

When bringing a multicultural awareness to an entire parish, it would be valuable to provide the parish staff with good catechesis on multicultural issues. It is vital to get as much support as possible from all the key players in a pastoral team—including the pastor, the liturgy team, the religious education office, and even the school principal—in the hope that most of them will agree and support the sharing and celebrating of different cultures at various levels. Without this consensus, the promotion of multicultural liturgy and liturgical music may become an imposition from above. In fact, the ideal would be that the entire parish comes to support this sharing of cultures and that everyone can celebrate it in liturgy.

Some of our early multicultural liturgical experiences arose when the dominant culture recognized and admitted the presence of one or more additional cultures within its midst. That simple recognition of others is crucial and, for some, a very fine starting point. Once that recognition is made, a typical procedure is an invitation to all cultural groups to celebrate a common Mass in which music groups of the various cultures are each assigned a song during a certain portion of the liturgy. And so, for instance, a Spanish-speaking music group gets to sing the entrance song, and a Vietnamese-speaking music group sings the music at the preparation of the gifts, while an English-speaking music group leads the rest of the Mass. While this demonstrates goodwill, it is also evident that the mere juxtaposition of songs in different languages does not reach the ideal of a truly *multicultural* liturgy.

The prophet Isaiah provides an image of the ideal multicultural celebration: the so-called "peaceable kingdom," in which

> Then the wolf shall be a guest of the lamb,
>   and the leopard shall lie down with the young goat;
> The calf and the young lion shall browse together,
>   with a little child to guide them.
> The cow and the bear shall graze,
>   together their young shall lie down;
>   the lion shall eat hay like the ox.
> The baby shall play by the viper's den,
>   and the child lay his hand on the adder's lair.
>   (Isa 11:6-8)

This is what the reign of God will look like, and to enter this reign of God we must be willing to enter a world different from our own. Because we have put on Christ, and Christ has taken down the walls of division, approaching the ideal multicultural liturgy is very much like approaching the fullness of the reign of God. So by singing a song in the language of other cultures, we step into the world they inhabit. This is good practice for stepping into the reign of God. And, just like life, we don't always do this perfectly. We are often drawn *through* our fears, our mistakes, and insecurities into the reign of God. It really is about sharing in a foretaste of the reign of God, setting aside our own individual needs and giving priority to the needs of the entire assembly.

One of the expectations of multicultural liturgies is that everything will be perfect and that everyone will fully understand what goes on. The challenge of the practical application, however, involves people coming to terms with giving up (for a time) their own complete nourishment and individual needs to understand everything. For example, individuals may feel uncomfortable with a different language, with different musical rhythms, or even with people clapping their hands or dancing at liturgy, but they are asked to take part in some of these rituals during a multicultural celebration.

Thus every parish that chooses to express its prayer life through multicultural liturgical prayer (even if it is only occasionally) also involves all its worshipers in the spiritual work of surrendering and letting go for the sake of a greater good. That is why having high expectations that everything will go smoothly from the start is unrealistic for everyone and could set people up for disappointment. It would be good to admit from the very beginning that multicultural liturgies may become a little bit messy, a bit challenging, even intimidating. But a good catechesis that focuses on celebrating unity in Christ in the midst of diversity will be most helpful.

It may be helpful for the parish to set up either a committee or an office to support multicultural liturgy. When I arrived at one parish, I found such a committee already in place and meeting every few months to decide on which celebrations to focus their energies. The multicultural committee would plan, execute, and evaluate various multicultural parish celebrations throughout the year. I found this so impressive!

It is always important, of course, to be patient with the process of introducing multicultural liturgy to a parish that has not yet enjoyed the opportunity. Both the leadership and the parishioners will need to keep in mind, once again, that the process of becoming a multicultural worshiping community sets them on a path of *conversion* from individual needs to patience and, ultimately, to self-emptying and unity through diversity. Therefore, everyone involved in the promotion of multicultural liturgy should model great patience and a renewed capacity to listen to the challenges that individual members of the parish face throughout the process.

Regarding the choice of liturgical music, the pastoral team will need to be in touch with its people—that is, the team must have a discerning sense of the makeup of the parish. This will help to determine the kinds of occasions to be celebrated as well as the kinds of multicultural music to be used. The goal here is that the music fits the occasion and that the occasion becomes a celebration for the *whole* parish to celebrate and express gratitude for God's saving deeds. It is possible, however, that some may initially find this sort of celebration threatening or so completely different that they are pulled out of their comfort zones. Still, the pastoral team will want to use every means—through education, encouragement, and well-celebrated liturgies—to let the liturgical experience speak for itself. All in all, the better the leadership has prepared itself and the parish, the more smoothly will these efforts bear fruit.

Composing and Programming Music for Bilingual Liturgies

When introducing a bilingual liturgy, do so in small increments. It would be wise first to use different languages with those sung parts of the liturgy that are so familiar that it would be difficult to get lost: penitential rite, the fraction rite (the Lamb of God), the response to the prayers of the faithful, or the sprinkling rite. One possibility would be to sing the common refrains in Latin or Greek and the verses in another language. The basic idea here is to choose a simple and brief acclamation that is tied to a liturgical action with which everyone is familiar.

Take the penitential rite, for example. Once the choice has been made for either a bilingual or trilingual response, all one has to do is figure out how to sing "Lord, have mercy" in each language, as in this example by Bob Hurd:

© 1988, Bob Hurd. Published by OCP, 5536 NE Hassalo, Portland, OR 97213. All rights reserved. Used with permission.

Another approach involves writing each trope in a different language (English, Spanish, Chinese, Filipino, etc.) and sing the common refrain in Latin or Greek. The combination of a familiar and ancient phrase—like *Kyrie eleison*—with the familiar ritual action will help people feel comfortable, at least to some degree.

Or the sprinkling rite, for example, could begin with a phrase in English like "Water of life, remind us of your love." The next phrase in Spanish begins, "*Agua de vida. . . .*" Then add a third phrase, say, in Vietnamese. As people sing in their own language they may feel a level of comfort that allows them to become more open to learning the language equivalents of what they already know is happening ritually. Knowing what is going on ritually helps a lot in this instance.

In multicultural music composition we call this "code switching"—that is, each language may be considered a code with its symbols for communication. Composers of multicultural music should be careful about making sure that the alternating of one language to another in a worship song does not leave anyone with an incomplete thought. There are many approaches to code-switching. One may use short phrases that are a translation of one another; one may have a full sentence in one language and then the same sentence in a different language; one may use a few words or short phrases that are obvious to all; or, in some cases, one may provide a translation in a footnote in the assembly score—or at least provide a translation in a rehearsal prior to worship.

The point is that although there are different situations regarding how we switch from one language to another, it is the responsibility of the composer of the text (and the music to some degree) to ensure that the thoughts are complete and make sense to those present in the liturgy.

Through patience and reflection, I believe we have become better at shaping songs that will aid worshiping communities to sing successfully in multicultural celebrations. Again, liturgists should not be too hesitant also to use Latin and Greek, especially when we are using the familiar texts in the Order of Mass.

Singing a familiar acclamation like the Sanctus challenges people to learn to pronounce words that may be unfamiliar but will make sense in the context of the sung acclamation.

When using a bilingual Sanctus the issue at hand is to find a musical rendering in which code-switching makes sense. Singing the Sanctus is quite easy compared to singing, for example, the Gloria. The number of words and syllables that it takes to translate from English into Spanish may become daunting even for a trained choir. Therefore, it may be best for a multicultural congregation to attempt to sing the first verse of the Gloria in Spanish, for example, the second in Filipino, the third in English, and include a short refrain with all three languages (or perhaps use the Latin for the refrain). We all know what we are saying when singing the Gloria. We know we are praising God. Therefore, we are already anchored in the liturgical action. Different cantors from the different language groups may also be invited to lead this song in order to model ministry in a multicultural setting.

Equally difficult is creating a composition for the responsorial psalm, especially because these change week to week. The text writer and composer will need to make decisions about what to say, what translation to use, how the languages will be alternated, and so on. All in all, know your assembly.

Music © 1999, 2009, Bob Hurd. Published by OCP. All rights reserved. Used with permission.

It is one thing to sing this in Red Oak, Iowa, and another to sing it in San Antonio, Texas. It is possible for groups to grow in their capacities to handle texts in other languages. It's all about time, effort, and the catechesis provided the assembly by the leadership.

The liturgy already uses other languages: Latin, Greek, and Hebrew. What we are doing now is simply expanding on the rich linguistic heritage and tradition of the church for the sake of expressing our oneness in Christ. Therefore, it is vital that individual communities do not get "boxed into" believing that their Mass is the center of the universe. Human beings, creatures of habit that we are, sit in the same pew, go to Mass at the same time, visit with the same friends, and condition ourselves not to notice when those different from us show up for liturgy. Bilingual or multicultural liturgy awakens us to the fact that the universal church—and possibly even our own local community—is much more diverse than we have noticed.

While introducing a multicultural hymn for a particular feast day, one may explain to the congregation: "Today we are singing this particular bilingual song because this coming weekend the church celebrates our Lady of Guadalupe. This is our way of connecting with our brothers and sisters and of showing solidarity with them. Let us remember how God calls all humanity into oneness in Christ." Then we would choose a bilingual refrain and sing all the verses in English (for the Mass in English) and all the verses in Spanish (for the Mass in Spanish).

The Spirituality of Multicultural Singing

The spirituality of multicultural singing has its foundation in the essential teaching of Jesus: dying to ourselves so that others may live. When we come to liturgy in one language or many, we are called to leave our own individual needs aside and think in terms of the collective needs of the community for a brief period. When we pour out our lives for the sake of others, our heart is open to hear God speak. Following Christ as our ultimate model, we give our lives so that new life may be given to the world. And through the Holy Spirit we receive the strength to continue the mission of the church in our everyday lives.

The sense of spirituality here involves a growing recognition of the many others who are one in Christ (and growing may sometimes be painful). The body has many parts, yet it is one. This means that, as a Spanish speaker, I have had to learn Vietnamese because there are Vietnamese members in my choir and in our parish. It was both an exciting and a nerve-racking experience to learn a particular song in Vietnamese. The delight on the faces of the choir and of the assembly, however, confirmed the good we did as the sense of unity among the people of God became palpable.

Saint Paul writes to the Ephesian community:

> So then you are no longer strangers and sojourners, but you are fellow citizens with the holy ones and members of the household of God, built upon the foundation of the apostles and prophets, with Christ Jesus himself as the capstone. Through him the whole structure is held together and grows into a temple sacred in the Lord; in him you also are being built together into a dwelling place of God in the Spirit. (Eph 2:19-22)

This wonderful passage resonates with the experience of sharing worship with people from other cultures than our own. We are all made one in Christ, and we all dwell in the household of God. Let us celebrate our unity through our diversity!

6

Three Judgments, One Evaluation

John Foley, SJ

I have noticed a significant problem in the church's advice to parishes regarding music. I think it causes difficulty week after week, but few seem to notice and few do anything about it. The problem is this: according to the bishops, a threefold judgment is supposed to be made about the music used in every Mass in every parish in the country. The judgment should be *musical, liturgical,* and *pastoral*. But how often does this ever really happen?

I would like to approach this question through the last two documents on liturgy published by the United States Conference of Catholic Bishops. The first of these, *Music in Catholic Worship* (MCW), sets up the three judgments:

> To determine the value of a given musical element in a liturgical celebration a threefold judgment must be made: musical, liturgical, pastoral. (MCW 25)

The document goes on to elaborate upon each of these sections of the threefold judgment at a much greater length than can be developed here. But since MCW is an important precursor to the more recent document, *Sing to the Lord* (STL), I want to stress some of its highlights.

In the first place, why are these three qualities considered so important? Maybe it is because they answer so many of the manifold complaints one hears about Catholic church music—namely, that it is:

- too highbrow (not singable),
- too lowbrow (not good),
- just a show,
- ignorant of the traditions of the church (Gregorian chant, renaissance, baroque, Mozart, etc.),
- the performance of someone's personal spirituality (to the detriment of church doctrine),
- not sufficiently inspirational,
- dismissive of the congregation's participation,
- or too presumptive that participation merely means "everybody singing."

Different factions each have their own stake in the discussion. Often, I have noted, the result is not cooperation but competition, with the prize being conversion to only the liturgical music style that goes along with the belief of one or the other type.

But let us look at the three judgments and see if they speak at least to the complaints I have sketched above.

First, in its section on "The Musical Judgment" MCW asks: "Is the music technically, aesthetically, and expressively good?" This may be a frightening question. The document then quotes St. Augustine in order to soften the impact: "Do not allow yourselves to be offended by the imperfect while you strive for the perfect." Then MCW lists the following types of music as suitable for Mass: chant, polyphony, choral hymn, responsorial singing, contemporary composition, and music in the folk idiom.

Second, structural advice is provided in a section on "The Liturgical Judgment." What is the *impact* of different musical parts? For example, if the entrance song, Kyrie, or Gloria are too elaborate they may outdo the proclamation of the Word. Or, if an offertory song is overly ornate and is followed by a spoken Sanctus, the eucharistic prayer may seem denigrated. Liturgical expertise requires balance.

The document goes on to delineate various roles involved in the liturgy: the congregation, the cantor, the choir, and the organist—including the placement of the organ.

Finally, in its section on "The Pastoral Judgment," MCW specifies that:

> The pastoral judgment governs the use and function of every element of celebration. Ideally this judgment is made by the planning team or committee. It is the judgment that must be made in this particular situation, in these concrete circumstances. Does music in the celebration enable these people to express their faith, in this place, in this age, in this culture? (MCW 39)

There is brilliance in the delineation of the three aspects. Quite obviously, any parish that skimps on one or the other will dramatically decrease the effectiveness of the eucharistic liturgy. To be quite candid, it must be admitted that in the United States only one judgment is usually applied in choosing music for Mass, or at most two. This is a problem.

But let us imagine, for a moment, a church where all three aspects are well considered and brought together. Such a church would obviously exclude music that is simply someone's favorite but lacking in excellence. And its members would bear in mind that quality is judged within the type and form of music under discussion, not by standards typical of some other genre. Bach did not write in the folk idiom; popular hymnody should not be subject to the same rules as chant or polyphony.

To summarize, music has to be well written and it has to *work* in the liturgy. Mere insertions into the liturgical structure are not advisable; each piece should support the ritual movement of the Mass, consist of settings of the actual words of the ritual, and fit gently into the type of singing that this particular parish finds helpful, prayerful, and ritually fitting—as opposed to something forced down their throats, so to speak.

So how may we choose music that satisfies all these goals?

Getting Practical

Naturally, these three judgments beg the question: *who makes these judgments?* Is it the pastor? Or the choir leader? Or the liturgist—if there happens to be one on staff? Or the priest who is presiding that day? Do they each make their own decision and then fight it out? More diplomatically, how are these various sets of expertise supposed to come together in each and every Mass? Before you come to an easy answer, remember that STL is very clear in saying that "what is to be sung at the Liturgy . . . is ultimately the responsibility of the pastor and of the priest who will celebrate the Mass" (STL 119).[1] The specter of an otherwise good-willed priest completely reorganizing the musical, pastoral, and liturgical practices of his newly assigned church should alert all presiders to the warning from STL: the priest "should have in mind the common spiritual good of the people of God, rather than his own inclinations" (STL 119).[2] But, indifference to inclinations or not, the document still places the burden of all three judgments squarely on the *pastor's* shoulders. It is he who is expected to know the pastoral area, *as well as* the liturgical and musical. Of course this is asking a lot!

One solution might be for a parish to diversify its resources. That is, a parish could hire those with expertise in *each* area: a choirmaster, organist, or keyboardist for the musical judgment; a liturgist to oversee the constantly varying progressions within each liturgy and within the liturgical year; and a pastor to look after the pastoral dimension. STL allows for this, albeit in rather mild terms: "The pastor *may* designate that the director of music or a Liturgy or music committee meet regularly to make the preparations necessary for a good use of the available liturgical and musical options" (STL 120, italics mine). The key word, however, is *may*; this may or *may not* happen. And there is no provision for specific liturgical knowledge. A more pragmatic solution is needed here, and not just one in which the priest *may* seek help from experts or committees if he is really strapped. He needs help from them *always*, not just once in a while.

With this in mind, perhaps the three judgments are more trouble than they are worth. Is there *really* a way to hire the right people and coordinate their judgments each week?

Looking Closer

Let me suggest a starting point, one based on an example from the US Constitution—no matter how far it might seem from the subject at hand.

When the US Constitution was nearing ratification, a series of articles defending that document began appearing in a number of newspapers. Scholars believe these articles, called *The Federalist Papers*, were written by Alexander Hamilton, James Madison, and John Jay. Theirs was a monumental task, of course, and comparison to the much more restricted purpose of this chapter may seem jejune. But theirs is a wisdom I hope to draw upon. Three discrete branches of government, with their relevant separation of powers, were under consideration with the idea that they would gather into one governing body. Likewise, we in the church are faced with three distinct judgments that are supposed to come together into "one evaluation" (STL 126).[3] How did our governmental predecessors handle the problem? By a system of *checks and balances*:

> An elective despotism was not the government we fought for; but one which should not only be founded on free principles, but in which the powers of government should be so divided and balanced among several bodies of magistracy, as that no one could transcend their legal limits, without being effectually checked and restrained by the others.[4]

Each branch of government is important and free, but each guards the provenance of the other. Each branch—legislative, judicial, and executive—carries out its own duties but also cooperates with the others.[5] We find separation but cooperation between powers. Congress may not enact just any law it pleases. The judicial branch oversees that law's congruence with the Constitution.

The president may not order any actions that strike his fancy. He would ordinarily have to seek the approval of Congress in order to declare war, in spite of the many ways around this provision. The Supreme Court is balanced by the fact that the president appoints them, and Congress must approve the appointments.

In other words, the founders reintroduced an ancient and clever principle called the "balance of powers," whereby each branch's decisions are checked by other branches, and balance is achieved.

Can we do the same? Can a parish check-and-balance the musical, liturgical, and pastoral powers in the selection of appropriate music?

First, let us look at how things can get out of balance. Take a church in which music performance has been very strong for a long time, for instance, and the musician in this program easily makes his or her own judgment as to what music to use, with little to no interference. The pastor must believe that such a musician has the pastoral and liturgical training necessary, in addition to the musical expertise, if he is to follow what the bishops say. But what if this is not the case?

Second, another danger is illustrated in the battle between enthusiasts for one or the other particular style or type of music. At least one of the forces (but not the only one) vying for control is that of classical and neoclassical music—that is, the opinion that where Palestrina is played, there is liturgy. To proceed on one musical principle alone, however, one must dispense with others. Likewise, the surge of folk masses, sometimes called "popular music masses," has illustrated very well the triumph of one style of music over the others, and over the other judgments urged by the bishops.

Third, there may be an exclusive attention to ritual at the expense of music and liturgy. Granted, the ritual words are of great importance in the Roman Catholic Mass, and music for Mass should always include them. Nevertheless, important questions arise: Is the music also truly apt for the congregation? Does it seem pastorally appropriate to this particular church of people, or will it reduce them to being merely observers of the splendid rite unfolding before them and without their active participation?

Finally, what about an exclusively pastoral approach? Imagine a parish that does not think much about its music because it invariably uses tunes that people like. As in the old-fashioned Broadway musical, people leave the church humming their favorite piece from today's Mass. That music may well have overshadowed the real meaning of the Mass. Where is the check and balance on such an easy way of proceeding?

The answer to this question is the same for each of these scenarios: the checks and balances are in each of the other judgments. There must be a way to include all three judgment areas, each working in harmony with the other and with restrictions on the others, with a real, palpable effect. Each area should be a check and a balance.

Applications

Alas, however, this may not necessarily work very well. Many churches lack all three forms of expertise: a pastoral expert, a liturgical savant, and a musical master. Parishes are far too strapped financially to afford even one specialist, let alone three.

Let us imagine that St. Albertino di Acquitrino parish (SADA) is fortunate to have a rather large congregation of interested people. Its pastor is a sensitive man with a good intuition in pastoral matters. Two choirs sing regularly under a director who has had academic music training. And—miracle of miracles—a woman named Mildred resides in the parish and received her master's degree in liturgy from Notre Dame when it was at its zenith. SADA has a most fortunate situation. How could Masses turn out anything but the ideal?

Quite easily, I'm afraid, if there is no mechanism to bring the judgment area and experts together. A time-honored method is the committee meeting. Priest, musician, and liturgist, each having done his and her work ahead of time, convene, discuss, and make decisions *together*. Like the elements of the US Government, each person supplies one resource only, that of the job for which each is present. Pastoral concerns are most important in any Mass. How quickly are the people being asked to learn new music? Are they able to do it? These are pastoral questions and must be given room. Yet the musician will check (that is, oppose) the pastoral temptation to select four or five favorite tunes, pleasing to all, plus a too familiar setting of acclamations.

The liturgical officer will make suggestions about the season of the year, the theme of the Mass, the flow of events both within the Mass and within the season. She will not allow these to be contravened, since without them the result will be "just one more Mass" with beautiful and attractive music, but lacking the major motivic force of all liturgy: ritual *relevance*. And the musician will represent the *quality* of liturgical pieces, seeking to keep both participation in and excellence of the music at the forefront.

Will there be mistakes and misfires in this seemingly perfect situation? Of course. But the purpose of these three competences is to arrive at a consensus in which creativity, rather than argument, is the goal.

Ways of Imperfection

But enough of "perfect" conditions. We all hope for them, but let us be realistic. Most parishes find themselves with few if any of the judgment areas covered. The priest balances counseling, homily preparation, and church business amid multiple other tasks, and he does not have the time or energy for meetings about the music. The musician(s) scrambles each week not just to choose the music but to prepare it and perform it. And there is one element almost universally missing from parishes: liturgical expertise. Who will make the liturgical judgment? Who actually knows enough about ritual and liturgical principles, laws, and practices to provide that check and balance? Usually the answer is something like, "Oh, we make our way along, and really it is just a matter of following the instructions in the book." If this were true, there would be no need for the liturgical judgments! But, in fact, it is the most sophisticated, necessary, and subtle area of the three.

It must be noted that any of the three areas (or all of them) can be completely missing in a parish. We have to admire the Order of the Mass for standing up under these kinds of conditions.

One solution to this seemingly endless problem is to hire a trained liturgist to come in just once a month to help with the planning for the coming weeks of Sunday liturgies. Dioceses may see the value in such an arrangement and provide such a person (or persons) to go from parish to parish. With or without the diocese, however, someone might set him or herself up as a liturgical agent and serve a number of parishes as an advisor with a modest stipend. It is a win/win situation: the parish receives much needed help, and the liturgical agent can make a living.

As regards the musical judgment, however, things become more complicated. So much depends on the personal taste of the lead musician. Which style is the *right* one, and what pieces fit within it? This much can be said without doubt: unless your parish has a qualified and widely talented musician, there is a need for further training. Yes, this would mean dollars, but how much would it be worth for you to have a Mass each Sunday that fosters faith, plays out the paschal mystery within us, and crafts it with the knowledge of who we are as an assembly? It seems to this writer that this should be a major expenditure for any parish.

I have not yet mentioned the pastoral area because its content is not so easy to describe. Ordinarily this expertise would come from the priest or pastor himself. Above all, he would be likely to know the people of the parish and what works for them. How does music nurture the assembly? What music will aid these particular people in entering the paschal mystery to receive the active presence of Christ within it? I have in other places described this delicate sensing of the people as the "art of the assembly":

> [The pastoral person] must know the assembly and its contours like a midwife knows the mother. Years of musical practice and training can never make up for a lack of this.[6]

The art of the assembly is a particular, intuitive consciousness of the people's identity. What would be needed this Sunday to bring home liturgical and musical judgments for these, our own people—as opposed to those in other parishes who presume that their blog posts apply to all situations?

Another solution is to make a checklist. What if your parish—with all its plusses and its minuses—could organize its questions about each aspect of the liturgy around the three judgments? Liturgical questions might include: Does one section of the rite outweigh a more important one because of the music or the excellence of the homilist? Is there a buildup that leads the assembly to sense their oneness in the paschal mystery? How might all this work? Is the music mainly entertainment, or is it influenced by the liturgical and pastoral aspects?

Pastoral questions might include: Does this Mass fit these real people, or are they supposed to do all the adjusting? Are we leading the people or simply "doing our job" and never asking whether the people really understand in their hearts? Have we considered asking the entire assembly how the Mass, the music, the homily, the ritual build, and the *feel* of the liturgy come across? If not, why not?

And, finally, musical questions may include: Are we including music that is easy enough for the people to sing? *Do* they actually sing? Does the music approach excellence? Is music just a required addition to what is, after all, *just* the Mass? Or does the music aid and abet the other two areas? Any parish in the world can prepare a survey for the people—especially if they pass out pencils with each copy—to find out everything they need to know.

Most important, there would be a check box to say whether or when the major ministers of each area have *ever* taken a

Sunday off and sat in the pews to see, hear, and feel how the liturgy comes across. And if they have never done this, why not?

Such a checklist, more extensive and practical than what I have suggested thus far, could lift the liturgy and the music on the wings of the three judgments and fly toward one evaluation. The work of constructing such a list remains to be done, but who could be against it? Who would dare contest the right of the bishops to ask for *three* aspects to liturgical music, not just one?

But What Is the Point?

One otherwise unnoticed difference in the two documents is the arrangement between the three judgments. Whereas MCW had "musical, liturgical, pastoral" (MCW 25), STL arranges them with liturgical first, pastoral second, and musical third (STL 127–36). In the present author's estimation, this change was made simply to emphasize the fact that the pastoral and liturgical judgments lead up to and inform the musical.

The writing of *Sing to the Lord* required much discussion on unification. If there were three judgments, how could one judgment result? As a member of the advisory committee that composed STL, I can say that the answer did not come easily. We thought of saying that there is one judgment with three aspects, but it was felt that this would deemphasize the high importance of each aspect, thus making a decisive break with MCW. In the end, we judged that the best way was to introduce a new term: *evaluation*. If evaluation means the act of considering or examining something in order to judge its value, quality, importance, extent, or condition, then evaluation is the overarching notion, summing up within itself the judgments necessary for overview. The job of relevant church ministers is to *evaluate* the music for a given liturgy, using (and not omitting) the three judgments elaborated in MCW and STL.

But there is a deep and important reason for spending time and money on the three judgments. The church believes that Mass is a sacrament and a sacrifice, that these two are not to be separated, and, most importantly, that the presence of the Lord in the rite of the Eucharist is nothing less than the presence of the entire paschal mystery. Such a presence is an active one—the reality of Christ's accomplishment in his passion, death, and resurrection. The much-emphasized word *participation* means, first and foremost, participation in the paschal mystery rather than a social connection or a getting-to-know everyone else. How can each of the judgment areas contribute to this goal?

The Mass is a remembrance of Jesus' sacrifice on the cross, not just a memory. "Remember how grandfather used to wear that old hat?" This is a memory, merely a calling to mind events from the past. But a remembrance is based in the timeless reality of God. I ask the reader to follow this logic: God is a reality present at all times because God does not progress through time, but is himself the wholeness of time. He contains all of it, from beginning to end, all at once. Therefore, in God, the paschal mystery is not something that *was*, but rather something that *is* and remains *is* through all time. When an assembly steps into the sacred space of God's presence, they do not have to look back into the past to find the crucifixion or resurrection; these are present *now*, surrounding them, in God. Of course I do not mean a physical presence, as on the hill of Calvary, nor a reenactment of Christ's life as in a play, nor a mere memory that will help us straighten out our lives. In the Mass we are present at the sacrifice itself, timely in its timelessness. We are present by means of a sign of that which is truly present in the "always now" of God himself.

From this several conclusions follow. First, the liturgical judgment encompasses far more than asking the simplistic question whether all the rubrics are being followed. Rubrics are indeed important as minor instructions on the *how-to* of actions in the Mass.[7] Without denying any of these helpful formatting aids, however, it must be stated emphatically that the liturgical shape of the Mass exists to help the assembly enter into and imbibe the paschal mystery. Peter Fink's article, "Public and Private Moments in Christian Prayer," shows how people progress liturgically though the eucharistic liturgy from individuals into persons in community. The center of that community is the presence of the active Christ.[8]

Second, the pastoral judgment has the same goal but a different focus. Because congregations differ from each other, sometimes radically, the same solutions do not work for each and every church. STL says that musical ministers have to ask:

> Can a musical composition promote the sanctification of the members of the liturgical assembly by drawing them closer to the holy mysteries being celebrated? Does it strengthen their formation in faith by opening their hearts to the mystery being celebrated on this occasion or in this season? (STL 130)

Again, this particular talent, the pastoral one, by itself would probably be the most important of the three. As an illustration, many American churches get their success from the personality of the pastor together with his ability to know each person in the gathering by name and the problems and glories of each of their families. Who would not want such a home to go to each week?

The pastoral ability's very strength is a completely necessary factor in the Roman Catholic Mass. The pastor or priest may not be able to know every person in the congregation, since there are so many, but there is a way of knowing the people as a whole: their reactions, their likes and dislikes, the music they prefer. What it is that opens their hearts to the paschal mystery?[9]

Finally, the musical judgment refers to such a powerful element that some of the Reformation leaders (Huldrych Zwingli, for instance) forbade music in worship altogether. In their judgment, music distracted too much from prayer. Our question here would be a bit more modest: How may we harness music's power when it threatens to become more potent than the main goal? Mere modesty is not the answer. The paschal mystery is.

Most Catholic musicians have heard the maxim: Do not put the assembly's favorite hymn at the preparation of the gifts. Why? It is the only thing they will remember when Mass is ended. It displaces the dynamic of the Mass itself. Participation in the paschal mystery—that is, in the passion, death, and resurrection of Jesus—is the prime and exclusive purpose of the Eucharist. The whole assembly must be involved in accepting this invitation from God's hand. If a piece of music distracts from that gift, then such music is a danger to the Mass. The musical judgment deals not only with the quality of pieces of music but, much more importantly, the consonant help that music gives to the entire Mass as a harmonious sharing in the real presence of the paschal mystery.

I have outlined the very serious problem that lies at the heart of every celebration of the Mass: lack of skill (and perhaps even interest) in planning music for each Mass. This is contrary to the bishops' intentions and to common sense, so I have provided a few practical suggestions in the attempt to embed the three judgments and one evaluation into their source and foundation, the paschal mystery of Christ our Lord.

Notes

1. See also the *General Instruction on the Roman Missal* (GIRM) 111.
2. See also GIRM 352.
3. This phrase is a significant development upon MCW, which made no attempt to coordinate the three.
4. James Madison, *The Federalist Papers* 48. Online at: http://thomas.loc.gov/home/histdox/fedpapers.html.
5. In recent times the checks and balances have been seen to include the press—a "fourth power" that influences public opinion and therefore the action of the government branches. Add to this, for better or worse, the PACs (political action committees) that lobby congress, not without monies, each for its own particular cause. Comparison of these further powers with liturgical music, however, is beyond the scope of this essay.
6. John Foley, *Creativity and the Roots of Liturgy* (Portland: Pastoral Press, 1994), 269.

7. GIRM contains many more instructions, for the sake of practicality, that could be conceived as matter for the liturgical judgment.

8. Peter Fink, "Public and Private Moments in Christian Prayer," *Worship* 58, no. 6 (November 1984): 482–89.

9. One puzzle is MCW's statement, quoted earlier in this chapter: "Ideally this [pastoral] judgment is made by the planning team or committee" (MCW 39). Possibly a team or committee could have the collective sense of a congregations, but this seems less likely (at least to the present writer).

7

Composing for the American Church

Tom Kendzia

This essay is an attempt at a "how-to" document, employing the basic questions that govern any idea that has any hopes of being successful: Who, What, When, Where, and Why. While this approach may not seem esoteric or scholarly, I'm afraid this is what publishers are thinking when they look at music submitted for publication. We are in a field that is already overwhelmed with music, both old and new, for an American church that is composed of descendants of Western Europe, Asia, Latin America, Mexico, and Africa.

While the needs are many and varied, the existing repertoire attempts to fulfill the needs of a multicultural church at a time when the Catholic Church in America could not be more in flux in her styles of worship. A trip to ten neighboring parishes in any part of the United States will reveal that there is not one liturgical style in place among this growing, diverse church. And this reality is made more apparent in the diverse publications, worship aids, blogs, and public opinion that confront us in both the mainstream and religious media. There is, quite simply, not one way to worship in community within the Roman Catholic Church.

Let us look at the world that the publishers serve and the issues that they grapple with when reviewing a new composition. In the early 1980s, the so-called "golden-age" of contemporary liturgical music, I had the privilege of working for my first publisher, NALR, in the capacity of recording producer and engineer. One of the many varied tasks was to sit in on the review board of new music submissions. This consisted of mountains of cassette tapes and handwritten pages of all sorts of music, very often described in accompanying letters that the music came to the composers in their sleep! While I would not be willing to argue the DNA of inspiration, the tools needed to craft such an inspiration today are much more varied and complex than those in the early 1980s.

My own muses and influences have evolved since 1977, the year in which my first attempts at writing for the liturgy began. When asked to do a "memory-lane" concert at a diocesan event last summer, I revisited over thirty years of liturgical composition in order to decide what to include. Should I start with all the secular folk and pop songs that were commonplace in the post-Vatican II mass? Or do I dive right into the "Friends of the English Liturgy" (FEL) era? My earliest days of playing for Mass began in the late 1960s while in junior high school, as I played the organ and accordion as requested for the "lower" church masses, and then as I played the guitar in high school. The music of Ray Repp, Fr. Clarence Rivers, Joe Wise, Paul Quinlan, and others was the repertoire, as well as Peter, Paul, and Mary, Bob Dylan, and Lennon/McCartney. *Godspell* seemed sent from heaven for those looking for hip music for church! Many early 1970s church musicians would probably love to forget about including songs from *Jesus Christ Superstar* at Mass. And yet there are vivid memories of the Civil Rights marches of the 1960s and antiwar rallies where singing together helped to unite those involved and provide them with inner strength and peace. For my generation, "We Shall Overcome" became synonymous with the trials of that time. I personally heard Dr. Martin Luther King, Jr., proclaim in the midst of one of his most memorable and lasting speeches, "Over my head, I see Jesus in the air, there must be a God somewhere." Later in my own career this would change the way I would perceive assembly singing!

Who Sings? Everybody!

My own evolution as a composer since the late 1970s has taken me from a broad perspective of liturgical song to a more focused ideal of how music and ritual is integrated. Within the first year of graduation from college with a degree in music education and piano, I found myself working in a parish in suburban New York City in the city of Stamford, CT. The location is important to this discussion as the community that I served helped shape my earliest works. When I discovered that the parish folk group did a *Godspell* Mass every Easter, I knew that I had my work cut out for me, especially since at that point I had no formal training in church music. My experience of liturgical music was based on my childhood of organ and choir and then guitar Masses by the sixth grade. The music was so unlike the usual repertoire that people either loved or hated it—the latter especially when the organist and choir fell apart and was replaced by a well-meaning but inferior organist. Suddenly this new guitar thing took on a whole new life, and it seemed to speak to a new church. It sensed the connection between the Gospel and world events, such as the Civil Rights Movement and the Vietnam War. The human condition became intertwined with the liturgy, and the Mass seemed to become more vital, more connected to the immediate.

While attending a Catholic high school, the choir who sang at the school masses began learning the music of Fr. Clarence Rivers, which was vibrant and exciting, accompanied by a full band. We also sang the Mass parts, and everyone in the school was required to learn the music as part of religion class. Those classes incorporated pop music, such as "I Am a Rock" and "Bridge over Troubled Water," and helped break open aspects of spirituality and faith. The end result was a profound appreciation of sung music and faith formation. I began to understand that liturgical music needed to speak to and involve all who are praying together. I can recall meeting Paul Simon at a private party back in the late 1970s, and I remember his disbelief when I mentioned the use of his music within the confines of Catholic prayer and catechesis! This reality became my guiding force at a retreat where we sang popular folk songs at Mass together—priest, kids, musicians—and especially during the communion rite. It was perhaps the first time that the essence of Eucharist became real for me and all those present at this experience! And while the music was perhaps not even liturgical or eucharistic, the song "Day Is Done," made popular by Peter, Paul, and Mary, focused the presence of Christ from just the Eucharist to each other in community. It was powerful stuff for a bunch of high school boys, and I know that the memory of that experience continues to be the well I visit for a renewal of my own ministry.

I understood that music at Mass needed to be powerful, yet singable. It needed to be part of the Mass, not something that takes you *out of* the experience. And this knowledge would serve me well. It kept me focused on the needs of all gathered as one, all singing the Body of Christ into life.

At my first parish job as music director, I knew that I was expected to get everyone singing. Our resources consisted of a mediocre organ, a small, all-female choir, and a folk group of teenage girls consisting of a bunch of twelve-string guitars usually strumming the same strum for all the songs. The repertoire was based on the music of what was then known as the Missalette. There was little music in the music closet, save for a box of LPs and books by a number of current liturgical artists. After going through much of it, I found myself drawn to much of the music by the same artists—the St. Louis Jesuits. And after trying it on the folks in the pews, the reaction was very positive in that everyone seemed to enjoy singing the variety of styles. And the choir was able to sing in parts while assisting the song of the assembly. It was the success of this music that led me to begin writing in a contemporary, inclusive style. My understanding of this idea encompasses the use of all resources to engage everyone gathered, and the role of the music is subservient to the needs of the rites. If this is the guiding force, then the music is based on the singing and its needs. If the music is appealing, then all ages can relate as one voice. Singing the living body of Christ can then become a reality.

What gets sung? Everything!

Within the first year of that first parish job, it dawned on me that we needed a piano. While pianos are as common as an altar these days it was very rare to find one in a Catholic church back in the 1970s. Dr. Alex Peloquin, of the Diocese of Providence, RI, was the man responsible for using piano alongside the pipe organ in cathedral liturgy. Many of his compositions were scored for both instruments, and even though there is a heightened complexity to his writing style, he still wrote for everyone within his own resources. At the same time, his workshops encouraged pastors to get pianos in their churches. It is hard to remember that that was a shocking idea to many who saw it as vulgar and non-Catholic! The piano is now seen as able to accompany congregational singing better in music that is contemporary and rhythmic. Many composers in all styles are now writing music that has a distinct piano/keyboard part, and not an organ part, suggesting that the organist double the SATB voices in order to better support the vocal sound of the choir and the assembly. It is a very effective approach for improved singing to see the combined use of the piano and organ in the liturgy.

If the goal is always full, conscious, and active participation with the singing, then it would seem that we would want to try all styles of liturgical music in order to achieve that end. Not every composer may be comfortable writing in all styles, yet it is still possible to appreciate compositional variety when working on your own music. I would like to think that my own evolution has helped me to provide better music for assembly singing, while at the same time keeping it musically interesting and liturgically sound. Sometimes it can seem like an impossible task, especially if it feels that all the requirements of good liturgical music begin to overwhelm the creative process. In some ways, writing music for the liturgy is not unlike writing a film score. A good score is meant to be at one with the video, enhancing and helping to develop the storyline. A solid score helps you to focus on the dialogue, underpinning the action as it develops. A worthy score pulls you into the film unlike any other device available. A *great* film score is varied in style, dynamics, form, and especially rhythms. This must also be true of effective liturgical music.

As a composer who has been involved in parish ministry since first being published in 1980, my own work has ultimately been shaped by the various communities served throughout the United States. It has also been shaped by many years of collaboration with other musicians, liturgists, teachers, clergy, visual artists, and liturgical dancers. Recent work in Ireland has helped me shape melodic ideas, while jazz and R&B have always found a home in my writing style. At one of our Composer Forum presentations, Alice Parker opened my eyes to the needs of a good, sound, singable melody. That advice aided my work in a profound way and provided a better appreciation of how powerful folk music, especially the African-American spiritual, can be. The catechetical nature of that music is without peer, and my recent work in the catechetical field has further reinforced how important *variety* is to the prayer life of any community. While it is still popular to employ diversity by offering liturgies that have distinct musical styles—9:00 a.m. traditional Mass, 11:00 a.m. contemporary Mass, 5:00 p.m. LifeTeen Mass, etc.—many churches are successfully employing the use of variety of style *within* each of their liturgies. This model has been my approach as a practitioner, and has helped to create a varied compositional style.

As we enter a time when the liturgy seems to be in the land of extremes (Pre-Vatican II, LifeTeen, liturgy without a priest, etc.), there lives a liturgical experience that strives to embrace a more human approach to "Do this in memory of me." When ritual is rooted in the profound ordinariness of these words, then music can emulate the real presence in a more tangible approach that does not rely totally on mystery but accepts actual faith-based experience. A look at any popular American hymnal will clearly illustrate that we are a church that sings chant and motet, folk song and African-American spiritual, rock rhythms and pop harmonies, scriptural paraphrase and poetic interpretation, litanies and hymns, rounds and ostinatos, the bombastic and the intimate. There is a great diversity that we have come to accept as our sung prayer, the repertoire of the American Catholic Church.

When do we sing? All the time!

The musical needs of the liturgy need to be fully understood by the composer before he or she can effectively write music that better enables the specific rite to come to life, puts the liturgical action into proper focus, and pulls a sung response from those gathered.

Within the liturgy there are many diverse needs and demands placed upon the music. In my experience, success happens when all the needs have been met, and everyone present "gets it," responds in song, and moves on longing to repeat the experience a week later.

Failure happens when music is used ineffectively. The documents tell of this reality, but we don't need a document to make this sad reality any clearer. Liturgical composers are often drawn to a variety of different sources for inspiration. However, if the desire to wed full singing to ritual is the goal, then variety becomes an asset rather than a boon. The many different needs of any given liturgy provide the composer with a multitude of options, especially when the varied needs of the liturgical year are thrown into the mix.

It has been said that chant is the perfect liturgical music for numerous and great practical reasons. As a composer of contemporary liturgical music, I would be foolish not to study chant and its capacity to simply sing the rites. This concept has had an effect on many modern composers who have outright employed existing chants in their new works. Dan Schutte's "Christ, Circle Round Us" is a lovely Advent setting of the *Salve Regina* employing a text based on the O Antiphons and with a new, original refrain.

Others have taken the liturgical manner in which chant is used and created new forms with ritual language and contemporary compositional techniques. My own attempts at crafting liturgical music that is designed to "sing the rite" include: "Lead Us To The Water," "Gather Us In," "Lamb of God/Taste and See," "Halle, Halle/Pentecost Sequence."

One of the chief elements of my compositional experience is my practical parish work over the past 35 years. Without this "in the trench" time, I would not have the musical voice that is mine. While other composers have been successful without actually "doing" church ministry, this work has totally shaped my repertoire as I discover new ways to assist the rites that we pray in our lives.

Many years ago, Elaine Rendler addressed a group at NPM and told us all to prioritize the music at a given liturgy and expect the assembly to understand what is important to sing, and focus on improving that element. Conversely, if singing was simply not happening in your parish, drop all music other than the Gospel Acclamation (Alleluia)! Though at first shocking, it of course makes sense. If folks can start to appreciate this unique presence of Christ in the liturgy through Word, and if we believe that our lives are changed by this Word, then our shout of joy will resonate as one voice of the gathered believers. I still refer to this great challenge in my own workshops, and I will often use the example of how something as simple as the wrong tempo can kill the excitement of the Easter Alleluia. We still fear energy in our music, assuming that it might be disrespectful, and borrow too much from non-sacred culture outside of the church. I fear that we have come to confuse the sacred with the pietistic. This does not mean that we need to resort to lounge music or conga lines for Communion. But when we witness the joy that comes from lively music and movement within assemblies that have been thawed from the deep freeze of stiff participation, we know that there is no return to the past, regardless of how many new rules and guidelines come our way. What we sing is so intrinsically like a film score that I would suggest study of this field to impact the success of liturgical song.

Where do we sing? It depends. . . .

Anyone who has studied the documents, attended liturgical workshops, or has had access to the many articles and books written over the past thirty years will have come to the conclusion that there is a basic understanding of the spots in which we sing when we gather for liturgy. While many practitioners have developed a personal approach to this based on their own abilities, resources, and needs of the community, it is still safe to say that if you attend Mass anywhere in the United States, you will come across a musical outline that is similar in scope:

- Gathering song
- Kyrie/Gloria
- Responsorial Psalm
- Gospel Acclamation
- Preparation of Gifts
- Eucharistic Acclamations
- Fraction Rite
- Communion Song(s)
- Closing Song.

This outline is fairly common and is one that is usually synonymous with "good sung prayer." If you are wondering what parts of the liturgy need your focus as a composer, then this would be the list of headings that you might use to organize your work. An understanding of the components of these parts of the Mass would be an asset as music for prayer should be in tune with what it is supporting. A working knowledge of compositional form needs to be developed as well to best serve the music that you wish to be sung by all.

Another important need is to use text that speaks to the ritual it is being used for.

Using the film score as example once again, we know that a great score helps tell the story we see and hear. It helps unite elements of the story, and it is believed by some that a common motif that continues throughout the film helps greatly in making the plot connected. We can see this similarity in the use of similarly themed eucharistic acclamations, as this practice has become common and normal in liturgy today. In fact, it would be seen as unwise to use acclamations from three different sources for the Eucharist that have nothing in common musically and therefore do not create a sense of unity within the prayer.

Even now we have some Mass settings that attempt to link *all* the sung acclamations in a similar style, but this may be too much. More important would be to find ways to sing through the specific rites themselves with one musical motif, as with the eucharistic prayer. New explorations using this model would use the varied elements of music to help create this experience. Using the same melodic and harmonic ideas to unite a specific rite might seem obvious, but you could also use other compositional elements as well, such as rhythm, both in accompaniment and in the textual use. Variety is the spice!

Within this discussion, it would be important to recognize the overriding effect that the liturgical year has on how one creates music for liturgy. All of the elements of music would play an important role here, such as color, dynamics, tempo, form, rhythm, and instrumentation. When looking at the vast amount of liturgical music in print today, it is easy to discover that there is not just one way to sing in church, and therefore there is not just one way to compose music for singing in church!

Why sing at all? Why not?!

This may seem sarcastic, but in all sincerity there was never a more important time for liturgical composition to continue and flourish. As the liturgy continues to become more intrinsic to the faith formation of a community, the need for more music that is catechetical in nature will also grow. We need to continue to develop styles that respect our past and lead us into the future. We need to attract poets who will help us speak the words that will sing of the church's mission, Gospel living, and the living Christ.

We must use a diversity of styles that matches the diversity of the people of God. We must avoid turning to the language of other beliefs that contradict our own beliefs. We must not be afraid of the music of any given culture, as it has much to teach us about the music in people's hearts. We must listen to the music in our hearts and from them draw out, like the wise householder, treasures both new and old. When our music and our prayer have become truly integrated, so that it seems unnatural to have one without the other, then we will be able to say that we have achieved our goal!

Contributors

Cyprian Consiglio, OSB Cam, is a monk of New Camaldoli Hermitage in Big Sur, California, where he currently serves as prior of the community. An internationally known performer, recording artist, and composer, he has numerous collections of original sacred, world, and liturgical music to his credit. A student of the world's spiritual traditions, he has offered retreats and conferences around the world and authored articles for several books and periodicals. He has recorded and published numerous collections of sacred, world, and liturgical music. He is also the author of *Prayer in the Cave of the Heart* and *Spirit, Soul, Body*, both published by Liturgical Press.

Jaime Cortez is a pastoral musician from the Diocese of Phoenix, where he has served in various roles for over 25 years. He is currently the director of music and liturgy at Holy Cross Catholic Church in Mesa, Arizona. He has written some of the most beloved songs in Catholic liturgical music, including "Rain Down" and multiple songs that allow English-speaking communities to worship together with Spanish-speaking communities. Among his most well-known bilingual hymns is "Somos El Cuerpo de Cristo/We Are the Body of Christ." Jaime holds a bachelor's degree in Music Theory and Composition from the School of Music of Arizona State University.

John Foley, SJ, received his PhD in liturgical theology from the Graduate Theological Union in Berkeley. He founded the Center for Liturgy at Saint Louis University in 1993 and served as its director for over 18 years. Fr. Foley is a well-known liturgist and composer of liturgical music (e.g., "Cry of the Poor," "One Bread One Body," "Come to the Water," "May We Praise You," "For You Are My God," "Keep Me Safe O God," "Dwelling Place"), with more than 150 liturgical hymns in print. Many of his compositions were written during his membership in "The St. Louis Jesuits," a group of renowned liturgical composers. Currently he is Artist in Residence in the Catholic Studies Program at

Saint Louis University and editor of SLU's weekly web magazine *The Sunday Web Site* (liturgy.slu.edu).

Columba Kelly, OSB, is a Benedictine monk and priest of Saint Meinrad Archabbey in St. Meinrad, Indiana. He earned a Licentiate in Sacred Theology (STL) from Pontificio Ateneo Sant' Anselmo in 1959 and a doctorate from the Pontifical Institute of Sacred Music in 1963. In 1964 he was appointed choirmaster for Saint Meinrad Archabbey. Some of his works are available from the GIA, Oregon Catholic Press, and the website of the Saint Meinrad Archabbey.

Tom Kendzia has been a liturgical composer and musician for 35 years, with over 100 pieces of music published by Oregon Catholic Press (OCP). He holds a BMus in piano and music education from Manhattanville College. His professional work takes him throughout the world performing, teaching, and conducting master classes for musicians, liturgists, and catechists. He has been the music director at Christ the King Church in Kingston, Rhode Island, since 1986.

Lynn Trapp holds a distinguished career in the United States and abroad as concert organist, choral conductor, pianist, clinician for conferences and conventions, composer for several major publishers, liturgist, and author for pastoral journals. He holds degrees from Southern Illinois University (BM), University of Notre Dame (MM), and University of Kansas (DMA). His career archives are established in perpetuity at the Hesburgh Library at the University of Notre Dame.

Steven C. Warner is the founder and director of the Notre Dame Folk Choir at the University of Notre Dame, where he has been a member of the campus ministry staff since 1979. His sacred music is published exclusively through World Library Publications (WLP), and he has composed two of WLP's principal mass settings for the third typical edition of *The Roman Missal*: the *Mass of Charity and Love* and, with Karen Kirner, the *Mass for Our Lady*. In 2008 he was recognized as the Pastoral Musician of the Year by the National Association of Pastoral Musicians (NPM).

Credits

"Now Let Us from This Table Rise," lyrics by Fred Kaan © 1968 Hope Publishing Company, Carol Stream, IL 60188. All rights reserved. Used by permission.

"O God Beyond All Praising," lyrics by Michael Perry © 1982 The Jubilate Group (admin. by Hope Publishing Company, Carol Stream, IL 60188). All rights reserved. Used by permission.

"From Ashes to the Living Font," text © 1994 World Library Publications, wlpmusic.com. All rights reserved. Used by permission.

"Señor Ten Piedad," © 1988, Bob Hurd. Published by OCP, 5536 NE Hassalo, Portland, OR 97213. All rights reserved. Used with permission.

"Gloria" on p. 57, Spanish text © 1975, 1991, Comisión Episcopal de Pastoral Litúrgica de la Conferencia del Episcopado Mexicano. All rights reserved. Sole US agent: US Conference of Catholic Bishops. Used with permission. Music © 1999, 2009, Bob Hurd. Published by OCP. All rights reserved. Used with Permission.

English "Gloria" and "Holy" on pp. 10–11, Music by Columba Kelly © Saint Meinrad Archabbey 2011. All rights reserved. Used with permission.

Various musical compositions from the *Liber Hymnarius* and *Graduale Triplex* © SAS La Froidfontaine—Éditions de Solesmes, 1 pl. Dom Guéranger 72300, Solesmes, France. www.solesmes.com.

Excerpts from the English translation of *The Roman Missal* © 2010, International Commission on English in the Liturgy Corporation. All rights reserved.

Scripture texts in this work are taken from the *New American Bible, revised edition* © 2010, 1991, 1986, 1970 Confraternity of Christian Doctrine, Washington, D.C., and are used by permission of the copyright owner. All Rights Reserved. No part of the *New American Bible* may be reproduced in any form without permission in writing from the copyright owner.

Excerpts from documents of the Second Vatican Council are from *Vatican Council II: The Conciliar and Postconciliar Documents*, edited by Austin Flannery, OP, © 1996. Used with permission of Liturgical Press, Collegeville, Minnesota.

www.ingramcontent.com/pod-product-compliance
Lightning Source LLC
Chambersburg PA
CBHW051955290426
44110CB00015B/2252